The Psycho-Social Aspects of Stress Following Abortion

Anne Speckhard

Sheed & Ward

Sheed & Ward TM is a service of National Catholic Reporter Publishing, Inc.

Library of Congress Catalog Card Number: 86-63589

ISBN: 1-55612-059-1

Published by:

Sheed & Ward
115 E. Armour Blvd., P.O. Box 414292
Kansas City, MO 64141-4292

To order, call: (800) 333-7373

Contents

List of Figures

iv

Acknowledgements

No endeavor is ever an individual effort, and no success can be claimed without also acknowledging a debt to those others whose support made success possible. For this work I owe a great debt to the 30 women who so willingly opened up their lives to scrutiny of this sort. Many of the women interviewed stated that the interview was the first and only time that they had ever shared the whole story of their pregnancy and abortion experience with another person. Their telling was sometimes painful and certainly it created a sense of vulnerability. To these women, I give my thanks. I am also grateful to the members of my doctoral committee: John Brantner, Harold Finestone, Geraldine Gage, and Richard Hey; all of whom were very supportive. Special thanks is due to my adviser, Pauline Boss, who has inspired me throughout my graduate studies and without whose help I would never have reached this point. I am also grateful to my colleagues at the Office of Population Affairs (U.S. Department of Health and Human Services), where I worked during the completion of my dissertation, especially to those who made comments, reviewed drafts, and were supportive through-out: Gerry Hendershot, Kathleen Arnold-Sheeran, and Wanda Franz. Thanks also to Patty McKinney, whose work in this area and whose comments gave me the confidence and insight to pursue the subject. A special thanks is due to my student colleague, Jill Margolis, whose sense of humor and keen insight kept me "on my toes." Thanks also to my husband, Daniel, whose unceasing encouragement kept me from giving up.

Introduction

Over the past two decades dramatic social changes have occurred regarding the public view of abortion. Once viewed as an illicit clandestine activity, abortion is currently a procedure which is both legal and highly visible. Accompanying these dramatic social changes, is a concurrent shift in research perspectives concerning abortion has occurred. Early research efforts focused on the assumed individual pathology of the abortion patient, the assumption being that the decision to abort was an indication of individual pathology which could be expected to continue after the abortion experience. This assumption gave way to a new perspective on abortion as legal and societal forces have changed the context of obtaining an abortion from one of needing a medical or psychiatric reason to that of a private decision.

The theoretical shift over the past two decades was made from theories emphasizing individual pathology, to theories that viewed abortion as an adaptive coping response to the stress of unwanted pregnancy. Contextual variables were increasingly emphasized, particularly in relation to the decision making aspects of the abortion experience. Luker's research, in particular, highlights the shift to contextual factors by noting that women making the decision to abort made reference to their social, family, economic, medical, religious, and historic contexts. Luker's research demonstrated that the decision to abort clearly does not occur in a vacuum, nor does it arise out of individual pathology. Rather, the abortion decision was shown to be a contextually based activity engaged in as a means of coping with stress (Luker, 1975). As the research literature increasingly portrayed abortion as a coping mechanism, outcome studies increasingly shifted their focus to the adaptive outcomes of abortion, particularly to relief from the stress caused by unwanted pregnancy.

While the research emphases concerning abortion have changed over the past two decades, there remain glaring omissions in the research literature. The emphasis on the contextual nature of the abortion experience has been principally limited to the woman's decision-making phase. The abortion experience itself, and its outcomes for the woman, have not yet been studied within a contextual framework. Moreover, researchers have repeatedly segmented their efforts into examination of limited phases of the abortion experience (i.e. the decision making phase, the procedure itself, or its outcomes). No integrative model has therefore been generated that can adequately address the experience as a whole. In addition, the emphasis on abortion as a coping mechanism may prevent recognition of the potential dual roles of abortion. That is, while functioning as a coping mechanism, abortion also has the potential to act as a stressor.

Both effects of abortion (i.e. coping mechanism and stressor) are mediated by contextual variables. Thus at the inception of this research there was a need to examine in a contextual manner, the hypothesis that abortion may have dual roles, functioning both as a coping mechanism and a stressor.

The present research was conducted in order to explore the research question that abortion may function both as a coping mechanism and a stressor. A sample of women who had engaged in abortion as a coping strategy, but who were subsequently stressed by their experience of abortion, was assembled in order to confirm the hypothesis of abortion's dual roles and to explore and describe how abortion functions as a stressor. A contextual model borrowed from stress frameworks was employed to explore the experience of stress caused by abortion. Contextual data regarding many aspects of the pre- and post-abortion experience were collected in order to generate an integrative model of how abortion functions in its role as a stressor.

The current research is thus exploratory and descriptive. The resulting data are qualitative and interpretations generalize only to those women who are stressed by abortion. For purposes of this research, stress is defined in terms of the Boss model (1985) which emphasizes the perceptual nature of stress.

Over one million abortions are performed annually in the United States, with the majority of these being to young single women who may have limited access to coping resources. Although the proportion of women stressed by abortion remains unknown, this research lays the groundwork for beginning remedial and preventive efforts for those women who appear likely to experience abortion as a stressor.

Toward this end, there follows a review of the literature pertinent to abortion's role as a stressor, an overview of the research design and data collection, a report of the results, and discussion and summary sections.

DEDICATION

**To those women who unselfishly shared
their painful experiences for
the benefit of others.**

CHAPTER ONE
STRESS AND ABORTION:
AN OVERVIEW

Introduction to the Literature Review

Because the current research endeavor is more concerned with abortion's role as a stressor event than its success as a coping mechanism, we review only those studies that viewed abortion in its role as a stressor event. Many of the studies cited here contain a bias, rooted in psychiatric origins, that views women who decide to abort as pathological by definition of their rejection of their pregnant status. This bias is inherent in much of the literature pertaining to stress following abortion, which may limit the ability to generalize such studies to nonclinical populations of women. However, given the paucity of data concerning stress following abortion, this researcher felt it was important to include in the review those articles that made any documentation of the various manifestations of stress following abortion.

A less biased literature concerning stress following abortion, that will hopefully evolve in coming years, ought to be based on research that uses representative samples, or at least nonclinical samples, and that takes a more objective view of women choosing to abort their pregnancies. Such a view would take into account what Luker's (1975) research demonstrated—namely, that choosing to abort is a contextually based activity that involves the rational consideration by the woman, of the perceived costs and benefits of all alternatives she perceives as available to her.

Although the present research is qualitative and makes use of a nonrepresentative sample, it differs from the earlier more moralistically biased studies in two important ways. The decision to abort is viewed as a contextual versus a pathological activity, and no claims are made (as in earlier studies) that the results pertaining to women who are stressed following abortion necessarily generalize to all women who abort.

Over the last two decades research literature has shifted away from viewing the decision to abort as an indication of pathology to a view of abortion as an adaptive mechanism to cope with the stressor event of unwanted pregnancy. This theoretical shift is evidenced by the growing body of literature regarding the adaptive outcomes of abortion, principally relief from stress.

Abortion is indeed used by women as a means for coping with stress. However, abortion may also function as a stressor event. Conceptualized as a stressor event, abortion is best viewed in the context of current stress theories. Hill's $A + B + C = X$ model (1949) conceptualizes stress as the sum of the interaction of a stressor event with the perceptions of the event, and the resources available to cope with that event. Work by Boss (1985) has enlarged upon Hill's model to include the influence of six contextual areas (cultural, economic, religious, historical, developmental, and constitutional) which mediate the resources and especially perceptions regarding a stressor event, and thus the degree of stress experienced. Using these theories of stress, it becomes clear that to study abortion in its role as a stressor event, one must take into account the subject's perceptions and resources concerning the abortion experience and the contexts in which the abortion takes place.

Abortion is an experience that involves three distinct phases: decision making, the abortion procedure, and outcomes of the abortion. The majority of research concerning abortion's role as a stressor have examined abortion outcomes without reference to the decision-making phase, nor to the actual experience of the abortion procedure. Moreover, the degree of stress subsequent to abortion has generally been measured in terms of the degree of subsequent psychological functioning of the subject without reference to her social contexts prior to and subsequent to the abortion experience, her perceptions of the experience as they relate to her various social contexts (particularly familial and religious contexts), and her access to coping resources (both economic and non-economic). Thus review of the research literature regarding abortion's role as a stressor event yields only fragmented accounts of the larger experience. Because of this fragmented approach to abortion as a stressor, no integrative model has been drawn from past abortion research literature that adequately addressed the role of perceptions, resources, and social contexts as mediators of abortion's role as a stressor event.

Review of the Literature

The majority of research concerning stressful outcomes of abortion has conceptualized this stress in terms of psychological reactions which contain cognitive, emotional, and behavioral elements. Few studies have documented antecedent and subsequent changes in the woman's social contexts in relationship to her experience of abortion as a stressor. Thus the literature provides only one context (i.e. psychological functioning) in which to examine abortion's role as a stressor event. Although limited in theoretical perspective, the following reports contain a broad range of samples containing both clinical and nonclinical populations, as well as diverse age, ethnic, and social groupings of subjects experiencing post abortion stress.

Emotional Reactions to Abortion

Perception of abortion as a negative experience with accompanying emotions of sadness, grief, remorse, hurt and anguish is not an uncommon experience among women who have had abortions. Adverse reactions were seen in eighteen percent of one sample of women surveyed by psychiatrists. These women reported that they felt little or no relief and that they were overwhelmed by negative feelings. Even those women who were strongly supportive of the right to abort reacted to their own abortions with regret, anger, embarrassment, fear of disapproval, and even shame (Kent, 1977). "Negative emotional response (to abortion) involving guilt, sadness, or regret" is seen by some psychiatrists as a "part of the normal spectrum of response to abortion . . . Immediate negative response to abortion is not uncommon." Up to 43 percent of 500 women studied showed immediate negative response to abortion. The long-term negative response was as great as 50 percent. Up to 10 percent of women develop serious psychiatric complications (Friedman, 1974). In a second-year follow-up of fifty teenage girls, 24 percent described their abortions as a negative experience and indicated they would not have another abortion (Cvejic et al., 1977). "As many as one-fifth of the women allowed therapuetic abortions, later expressed regret for accepting the procedure" (Kolb, 1958). Careful follow-up of l09 teenage aborters revealed that "all of the girls had some sort of grief reaction," three of them required psychotherapy (Cowell). Anguish was the feeling reported by 384 women (73 percent of those questioned) who had undergone a legal abortion in Japan (Hayasaka, 1970). Upset and sadness were reported by a number of women interviewed shortly after their abortions (Osofsky and Osofsky, 1972). Anxiety following abortion was reported by 43 percent of women in one sample (Kent, 1977).

Guilt

Guilt is a frequently documented emotional reaction to abortion. In one study of women surveyed after legal abortion, 23 percent suffered severe guilt and 25 percent mild guilt, with symptoms including insomnia, decreased work capacity, and nervousness (Bulfin, 1975). Another study found that 26 percent of the women felt guilt after legal abortions (Kent, 1977). Guilt and other psychiatric manifestations following abortion were found in up to 55 percent of European women studied by psychiatrists (Simon & Sentuvia, 1966). Another study of 742 women questioned after abortion found that 87 were sad, and 73 cried and expressed feelings of guilt. Most of the women in this sample could not justify having an induced abortion and two-thirds of all those questioned said they would have given birth if abortion were still illegal (Osofsky and Osofsky, 1972). Of 84 women who had legal abortions and were visited in their homes about two years later, four were still embarrassed and distressed and didn't like to talk about it, nine were classified as consciously repressing guilt. Twenty-two had open feelings of guilt. Ten were classified as having suffered impairment of their mental health (Malmfors).

Clinicians have documented cases of women who functioned well before their abortions but subsequent to their abortions they experienced psychosis precipitated by guilt over the abortion. Spaulding and Cavenar (1978), who clearly have a psychiatric bias, state that "Even in our contemporary society, with relaxed sexual mores and widespread therapuetic abortion, some individuals do feel guilty about abortion. One may attempt to rationalize, intellectualize, or otherwise defend against guilt, but one cannot escape one's superego . . . "

Zimmerman (1977), who examined abortion from a sociological point of view, also found subjects suffering from guilt following abortion. Her explanation for the guilt, however, was based on the subjects' perceptions that abortion, although legal, was still not socially acceptable. Thus the subjects' perception of abortion as a deviant act, and the reinforcement for this perception from the women's various social systems, contributed to feelings of guilt following abortion.

The dilemma that occurs when abortion is legal but not clearly defined as a nondeviant act was also addressed by Blumberg (1975), although more from the point of the subject having to take individual responsiblity for defining whether or not the abortion was the right thing to do. He states that although the "right to choose'' in some sense frees, it also creates an awesome responsibility and sense of guilt sometimes associated with abortion. Guilt may arise from the woman's realization that she is responsible for a decision which must sacrifice some important goals and values (motherhood and the value of life) in order to sustain or attain other beliefs or achievements (career, self-determination, independence). Thus, when society increasingly accepted abortion as permissible, the guilt coming from that source (society) has been lessened, only to be ''at least partially replaced by an intrinsic awareness of responsibility'' which increased self-accusation and self guilt (Blumberg, Golbus, & Hanson, 1975).

Preoccupation with the concept of having allowed the abortionist to terminate their unborn child is a frequent manifestation of post-abortion guilt. One woman states it poignantly, ''Abortion killed my baby five years ago, I will never get over it'' (Anonymous, 1979).

Depression

Associated with guilt over the abortion is the tendency for women to become depressed after an abortion. The most prevalent psychological disturbances found in a study of 2,771 aborters were ''depressive personality developments with self-accusation and guilt complexes, fears of infertility, sexual phobias, and other symptoms resulting from unresolved conflicts'' (Saltenberger, 1984). Depressive reaction or post-abortal psychosis with hospitalization and/or suicidal attempt (including two deaths) befell 66 women in one study (Population Council Report, 1972). Depression, one of the emotions likely to be felt with more than moderate strength, was reported by 32 percent of women surveyed (Kent, 1977). Delayed onset of abortion related depression has also been reported. ''The significance of abortions may not be revealed until later periods of emotional depression. During depression occurring in the fifth or sixth decades of the patient's life, the psychiatrist frequently hears expressions of remorse and guilt concerning abortions that occurred twenty or more years earlier'' (Sands, 1973). Balter (1962) also reports that women who undergo legal abortion may develop, even years later, all sorts of emotional disorders which reach a climax with menopause.

Emotional Numbness

A less often studied but important psychological reaction to abortion is emotional numbness. Many women, particularly teenagers, seem to be unaffected by an induced abortion. But some psychiatrists believe this emotional numbness is also an adverse reaction, meriting psychiatric attention (Kent, 1977).

Summary of the Literature Review

Review of the literature concerning post-abortion stress reveals very little about the relationship of the stress to other variables such as the subject's perceptions concerning her pregnancy and abortion experience and her social contexts. Often the studies cited revealed a judgemental bias, rather than a sound research design. The tendency of researchers to view women choosing abortion as pathological, by definition of the subject's decision to abort, led to biased designs and biased interpretations of results.

Clearly, a more objective exploration of the experience of post-abortion stress in relationship to the woman's internal and external contexts would reveal a clearer understanding of how abortion acts as a stressor. Using the model of stress developed by Boss (1985), one would predict that the cultural, familial, religious, and economic contexts of a woman undergoing an abortion certainly might have an influence over the degree of stress experienced following abortion. Moreover the woman's perceptions of abortion, which stem from her philosophical, psychological, and sociological states, are also likely to influence the degree of stress experienced.

Although the research literature is informative in that it documents the psychological experience of stress following abortion, it is still undeveloped in its ability to explain objectively, without biased interpretation of findings, how abortion operates as a stressor event. Based on stress theory rather than moralistic bias, review of the literature clearly demonstrates a need for further research, particularly to explore the function of abortion as stressor as it relates to contextual and perceptual variables of the women experiencing post abortion stress.

CHAPTER TWO
RESEARCH METHODOLOGY

Design of the Research

The design of the present research is exploratory and descriptive. Its goal is to explore and describe abortion in its role as a stressor event. The theoretical orientation of this research contains concepts from family systems theory and from symbolic interaction, both of which are embedded in the stress models by Hill (1949) and Boss (1985). The present research is based upon these two models of stress.

Hill's ABC=X model of family stress defines the level of stress experienced as dependent upon the interaction of a stressor event (A), with the resources, (B), a family has available for coping, and their perceptions, (C), of the stressor event. Thus, according to Hill, variability in a family's access to coping resources and their perceptions of a stressor event explain the differences in the level of stress experienced by different families experiencing the same stressor event.

The contextual model of family stress by Boss (1985), built upon the earlier work of Hill (1949), emphasizes "the family's perception of the stressor event or situation as a major determinant of outcome" (i.e. coping versus crisis). Although the Boss model emphasizes perceptions, she states that the family's perception of a stressor event "is mediated by the context in which the stressful event or situation occurs." Thus the Boss model expands Hill's view of stress to include "family contexts from a social-psychological and biological perspective on both macro and micro levels of analysis" (Boss, 1985).

Although the Boss model deals with family stress in general terms, it was found to be very applicable to the exploration of the role of abortion as a stressor because it identifies the contextual variables that may influence the subject's experience of abortion as a stressor event. As mentioned in the review of literature, the research regarding abortion as a stressor generally has been limited to viewing abortion only in a psychological context. Thus, major research findings relate only to psychological variables as predictors or antecedents of abortion in its role as a stressor.

The present research seeks to expand current understanding of abortion's role as a stressor by taking into account other contextual variables, in addition to psychological, in order to broaden the view of abortion as a stressor for an individual embedded in a family system. The Boss contextual and perceptual model of family stress provides the framework and generic concepts necessary for such a task (Boss, 1985).

Although the Boss model is a family stress model and abortion is usually considered an individual stressor event, the present research viewed abortion as an event that is highly influenced by the social systems in which it occurs. Thus, although the present research had access to only one person in the system (because of the privacy issue), it was assumed that the woman's perception of the abortion event was based on significant others and those powerful enough to influence the meaning she gave to the event. Therefore, this researcher felt that the application of a family stress model to the study of post abortion stress was appropriate.

The following section will include definitions of the concepts inherent in the Boss model and will elaborate on how these concepts were applied to the study of abortion in its role as a stressor event. Figure 1 provides a graphic explanation of how the concepts identified in the Boss model interrelate to define the level and outcome of stress (i.e. coping vs. crisis). (See Figure 1 pg. 39)

External Contexts

The Boss model (1985) defines the external context of the stressor event or situation as comprised of six indicators: historical, economic, developmental, constitutional, religious, and cultural.

Historical Context

The historical context refers to the time the event takes place. For abortion research the historical context is very important. Recent changes in the manner in which abortions are obtained, performed, and perceived by the public have dramatically changed the historical context in which an abortion takes place today as compared to two decades ago. The most dramatic changes have occured since 1973 when the Supreme Court, in the Roe vs. Wade decision, liberalized the obtaining of abortion. Since the 1973 decision, women in all parts of the country have been able to obtain abortions on demand, as compared to having to demonstrate that the pregnancy was a danger to their health or well being. Moreover, abortion laws no longer limited abortions to the first trimester. Abortions became legally available throughout the entire nine months of pregnancy (Roe v. Wade Supreme Court Decision, 1973). Areas for this research investigation pertaining to historical context included the year the abortion took place, its legality, and the subject's perceptions of whether or not obtaining an abortion at this particular time was publicly acceptable within her community and social worlds.

Economic Context

The economic context refers to the state of the larger environment's economy. Since abortion is an economic good in the sense that it is a service that is both bought and sold, the economic context of abortion is also important to consider. Before abortion laws were liberalized in the early '70s, and when abortion was illegal, abortion was a relatively expensive service that limited its availability only to those that could afford to pay for it. As abortion laws were liberalized in the '70s, abortion services became more widespread and the costs became less prohibitive. Moreover, during the '70s, the court ruled that women eliglible for medicare could use these funds to pay for an abortion. However this ruling was struck down with the advent of the Hyde Amendment (1975) which prohibited the use of public funds to pay for abortions. Thus, although abortion services have become more widely available and less expensive, poorer women are still at a disadvantage in receiving abortion services.

The economic context of abortion must also be viewed in terms of how the cost of carrying a pregnancy to term and parenting is perceived. This is especially pertinent for young, single, pregnant women who are not financially supported by either their families-of-origin or the man who impregnated them. Public assistance for poor single parents is readily available, although it often does not cover the early prenatal period, a time when the abortion decision is usually made. Thus a pregnant woman may find herself financially assisted in the later months of pregnancy or following childbirth, while in the earlier months of her pregnancy she was left to fend for herself economically. Such an economic context would be influential concerning the decision to abort and perhaps also regarding feelings about the abortion once it had been performed.

The economic context of the abortion patient was thus to be explored both in terms of the stress caused by the expense of the abortion and also in terms of the economic considerations taken into account when the decision to abort was made.

Developmental Context

The developmental context refers to the state in the life cycle of both individuals and the family itself. Abortion patients are for the most part young women of college age, although women of all ages (that is within the childbearing range) are represented as abortion patients (Henshaw and O'Reilly, 1983). The age of the woman and her stage in her individual and family life cycle are hypothesized in this study to be influential to the degree of stress experienced following abortion.

Constitutional Context

The constitutional context of the family refers to the biological and physical strength of the members of the family. Because abortion is a medical procedure, the physical health and healing power of the patient are hypothesized to have some degree of influence over the degree of stress following abortion.

Religious Context

The religious context of the family refers to the religious beliefs of the family members as well as the beliefs of the religious body or social group that the family members have as their religious reference group (i.e. other Catholics, other Jews, etc.). Religious beliefs concerning when human life begins (i.e. at conception or some later point) and the valuing of the life of an unborn child in relation to the life of its mother, are related to how abortion is defined. Those religious groups that define conception as the point when human life begins and/or value the life of the unborn equally to its mother, are more likely to condemn abortion than those groups that see human life as beginning later in the pregnancy or at birth, and who value the mother's needs above those of the unborn. Because religious beliefs are often filtered through the family system, family and religious contexts may interact on the way stressful events are defined. The researchers found it pertinent to explore the religious beliefs of family members, of significant others, and of the abortion patient concerning abortion, to learn if these beliefs mediated the degree of stress experienced following abortion. In addition, religious beliefs concerning sexual behaviors, particularly the acceptability of out-of-wedlock sex, are considered important variables in how the abortion decision was made.

Cultural Context

The cultural context of the family is defined by Boss (1985) as that which "provides the canons and mores by which families define events of stress and their coping resources. The larger culture of which the family is part provides the rules by which the family operates at the micro level." Exploration of the cultural context of abortion, in this study, is specifically directed toward examining the woman's perceptions of the laws governing abortion in her community as well as her thoughts and feelings pertaining to the social acceptability of abortion in her community.

Internal Contexts

As Boss states, the six dimensions of the family's external context influence the family's internal context. The internal context of the family in stress is made up of three dimensions: the sociological, the psychological, and the philosophical (Boss, 1985).

Sociological Context

The sociological context refers to the structure and function of the family regarding its boundaries, role assignments, and perceptions regarding who is inside and who is outside those boundaries. Boundary ambiguity is a major variable in this regard. Under many conditions pregnancy is a time when a new family member is being welcomed into the family and adjustments are being made in how the family is to be structured and to function when the new baby arrives. In the case of an abortion, it was hypothesized in this study that there would be a period of ambiguity in the family's boundaries when it was unclear whether or not the fetus (or embryo) was to be admitted into the family's boundary. Abortion presumably is an indication that the new member is not to be admitted and the boundary ambiguity should be cleared up. Whether or not the boundary ambiguity does resolve itself in all cases or continues to be a stressor following abortion is of interest to this study.

Psychological Context

The psychological context refers to the family's ability or inability to use defense mechanisms when a stressful event occurs (Boss,

1985). Since denial and repression of awareness of one's sexuality have been documented as a "normal" occurence in many families and individuals where unwed sexual relations are occuring, it is of interest to this study as well. Denial or repression of the awareness of sexual behaviors on the part of the individual and the family system are hypothesized to create a context where abortion may be a logical coping strategy to deal with pregnancy in order for denial and repression to continue. An alternate hypothesis that cannot be tested with the present sample is that denial, continued beyond the point of safety for an abortion, could also operate to prevent abortion. Whether or not the use of denial and repression as strategies to cope with sexuality was functional versus stress producing for subjects in this study is to be explored.

Philosophical Context

The philosophical context of the family refers to its values and beliefs on a micro-level. Individual rules of the family can, for example, be different from the larger culture to which they belong (Boss, 1985). One of the areas of exploration for this study pertaining to philosophical context is the stated and implied rules family members held concerning how sexual behaviors and their outcomes were to be (or not be) communicated within the family system. In addition, the family's characteristic style of coping with stress was to be explored in relation to the stressor of abortion.

Summary of the Research Design

In summary, the objective of this research is to explore and describe abortion as a stressor event using the contextual model of family stress by Boss (1985). This model highlights the conceptual areas that need to be explored and described in order to result in a non-judgemental description of how abortion functions as a stressor and how contextual variables mediate abortion's effect on coping versus crisis behaviors.

Construction of the Interview Schedule

The interview schedule was constructed in stages, beginning with an analysis of the literature. Although the literature contained many references to stress following abortion, the majority of studies measured stress in terms of psychological dysfunction following abortion. This was useful in conceptualizing the range of individual psychological reactions to abortion, but was limited in the sense of a broader model of abortion as a stressor. The objective of this research is to address more than the psychological context of abortion as a stressor. The Boss model (1985) was used to generate questions that pertained to contextual variables other than psychological, which focus on stress theory more than on moral issues.

Interview questions were also generated by interviewing a panel of five professionals having expertise in abortion and reproductive issues and three women having had stressful abortion experiences. Panel members were interviewed in regard to the contextual variables that had previously been identified (from the literature and Boss model) to gain insights into their experience of abortion as a stressor. Comments from the panel, in conjunction with the research hypotheses, formed the basis for assembly of a preliminary interview schedule. This preliminary draft was circulated among panel members for further comments regarding wording and ordering of questions.

The interview schedule that resulted from the panel's final comments was subsequently submitted to pre-testing with five subjects who had had stressful abortion experiences. In pre-test interviews it became apparent that although the interview covered all of the contextual areas, questions needed to be more specific to the actual experience of abortion as a stressor event. Data from pre-test interviews supplied the necessary information for adding more specific questions to the original interview schedule. For example, it was learned in one pre-test interview that hallucinations and a feeling of being "haunted" by the aborted fetus were potential manifestations of post-abortion stress. Questions regarding these subject areas were thus included in the revised interview schedule. Without in-depth interviews during pre-testing, such questions may not have been included.

Following pre-test interviews, the final draft of the interview schedule was printed and ready to use. Although the in-depth open-ended questions predominated, fixed-choice questions were also included pertaining to specific manifestations of post abortion stress that had been identified in the pre-test interviews.

Sample Selection

The sample for the present research was selected with an intent to recruiting women who had experienced high stress reactions (self defined) subsequent to their abortions. Because the intent of this research is to learn how abortion functions as a stressor, only women who perceived themselves as having been highly stressed by abortion were recruited into the sample. Such women were identified by clinicians and other subjects who knew of the women's stressful abortion experiences, but in the end, their own definition of themselves as highly stressed was the critical criteria. When recruited into the sample, subjects were asked to take part in the research based on their subjective perception of having had a stressful abortion experience.

In general, abortion is a particularly sensitive topic, an event seldom discussed and rarely revealed to others by those who have experienced it. Frequently post-abortive women take deliberate measures to avoid the subject altogether. Thus in the discourse of everyday life, abortion as a personal experience is an action that the average person cannot be curious about (Zimmerman, 1977). From the onset in the present research, it was assumed that obtaining a sample of women who would be willing to talk about their abortion experiences would be difficult. It was only through the aid of clinicians and subjects themselves that women were identified who had experienced high stress post- abortion reactions and were willing to talk about it.

Recruitment of Subjects

Women who experienced high post-abortion stress were recruited into the sample through contact and referral from clinicians and other subjects, using the "snowball" technique. The initial referral sources were exclusively clinicians, but as the number of subjects increased, increasing numbers of subjects were referred into the research by other subjects. Although such a sampling technique may have resulted in assembling a sample of women who were connected in a social network, a check of the sample records revealed that subjects often had one other friend in the sample, but were unacquainted with any of the other subjects.

The process of recruitment began with the referral source verbally describing the research to the potential subject. If interest was apparent, the referral source gave this person a written description of the research (see Human Subjects Forms in Appendix A). If the woman then wished to participate in the research, she gave informed consent and permission for the referral source to give her first name and telephone number to the researcher. Verbal informed consent, rather than written, was requested in order to avoid the use of full names since the anonymity of subjects had to be guaranteed.

The decision was made to have the researcher initiate telephone contact with the subject once permission was given, instead of vice versa. This decision was based on the suggestion of the referral sources who felt subjects would be more comfortable with that arrangement. This also avoided long distance telephone charges acruing to those subjects who lived at a distance from the researcher.

Upon receiving word of a subject's desire to participate, the researcher contacted the potential subject by telephone. The researcher initially identified herself and her linkage to the referral source before mention was made of the purpose for the call. Once recognition occurred, the researcher proceeded to explain the research objective again and receive from the subject a verbal reaffirmation of informed consent to participate.

Once informed consent was attained, the researcher and subject arranged a convenient time for the forty-five minute interview to take place. Subjects living within reasonable travelling distance of the researcher were offered the choice of a face-to-face or telephone interview. The telephone interview was presented, based on the results of the pre-test interviews, as an option to preserve total confidentiality. At the time of the interview (which was immediate in some cases), the researcher reviewed the content of the interview schedule and reminded the subject of her right to discontinue the interview at any time and withdraw from the study without repercussion.

The researcher pre-tested this process with five subjects and found it to be satisfactory from the viewpoint of the subjects. All of the pre-test subjects expressed enthusiasm to participate. Despite some anxiety, they all expressed pleasure and relief in having someone listen to their entire story. It appeared that these women had often tried to talk to others about their experiences and had received only negative feedback. Thus they perceived the interview as mutually beneficial.

Although this reaction continued with the larger sampling, the human subjects precautions described above were nevertheless strictly adhered to.

Administration of the Research Instrument

Thirty subjects were interviewed over a three month time span from March 1984 to May 1984. The response rate for the study was 100 percent. Of all the women contacted by referral sources, all agreed to participate, and when contacted by the researcher, none of the women withdrew their original consent to participate. By request of the subjects, all but one of the interviews took place over the telephone for reasons of confidentiality and convenience. The one subject who requested a face-to-face interview did so based on the lack of telephone privacy in her home.

Initial contact between researcher and subject was usually for the purposes of introduction, explanations, reaffirmation of informed consent, and scheduling of a time for the interview to take place. Seven of the women indicated a desire to be interviewed immediately. This request was accommodated in all but one case.

Generally, the first contact between researcher and subject involved some degree of suspicion on the part of the subject. Although the subjects had received a thorough description of the research from the recruiting source, prior to giving their consent to be contacted, many subjects wanted to be reassured concerning how the interview data were to subsequently be used.

Suprisingly, subjects expressed more concern over the political use of the data than over having their own confidentiality honored. Feeling exploited by their abortion experiences, many of the subjects requested advance assurances that the purpose of the research was not solely to promote "pro-choice" causes. Assurance was given with an explanation of the desire to objectively present data concerning stress following abortion based on the results of these interviews.

Although concerns about confidentiality were not voiced nearly as often, the researcher made certain to assure subjects at the onset of the interview that personal data would be edited from the resulting manuscripts in order to preserve confidentiality. Interviews were tape recorded and permission to do so was sought before recording was begun. Assurances were given regarding the destruction of the tapes following transcription and analysis of the results. Subjects were reminded that they could withdraw from the research and discontinue the interview at any time.

Following these arrangements, the interview began with a brief overview of the purpose of the interview (i.e. to learn about stress following abortion) and the scope of the content of the interview. Before active questioning began, the subject was presented with the opportunity to tell her own story, in her own words, so as to foster collection of data regarding the woman's reality concerning her experience and avoid imposing the researcher's preconceived notions about it. In making this request, the subject was told that the researcher found it helpful to let the subject tell her own story in her own words before proceeding with the fixed-choice questioning. This request was made with the following subject areas outlined as a guide for telling her story: the circumstances under which she became pregnant, the manner in which the abortion decision was made, the experience of the abortion procedure itself, and her stress reactions to it. This proved to be a useful technique, as it provided a structure for gathering data on what the women themselves thought was important regarding their experiences. It also allowed them to add as much other information as they wished, which greatly increased the richness of data collection.

As the women began the interview by telling their stories, the researcher followed along on the interview schedule marking off areas that had been covered and checking those that still needed to be specifically addressed. Following the subject's narrative, the researcher began with the interview instrument, probing those areas that had not already been covered.

An interesting phenomenon that occurred with many of the subjects as they recalled and recounted the abortion procedure itself was their apparent testing of this researcher's willingness to listen to their story and the content of that particular experience. Having tried to tell others about their experience, many of the women had encountered negative feedback, and apparently were not willing to risk the same again. Thus, many of the women became nervous (as indicated by their self-reflecting comments and voice tone) when they approached the subject of recounting details of the abortion procedure. They expressed concern that they might not be able to recount it without an emotional outburst such as tears. The researcher reassured the subjects while reminding them to feel free to avoid discussion of this particularly sensitive subject area. Once reassured concerning the researcher's willingness to listen and accept, all of the subjects expressing such fears proceeded to recount this portion of their experience with little apparent difficulty (as indicated by voice tone and self-reflective comments). Thus it appeared that the subjects had a great deal of concern over being rejected by the listener for having had such an experience and for still having emotional reactions to it. Many of the subjects expressed great relief in having been able to tell another person about this portion of their experience and expressed gratitude later in the interview.

The interviews ended with the women being asked if they had further comments to add. If they wished, they gave their names and addresses in order to receive a summary of the results. All of the subjects requested a summary of the results indicating a deep curiousity regarding the experiences of other women. Many of the women expressed their gratitude for having the researcher listen nonjudgementally to what many termed "the first time I have ever told one person my whole story" and for having had the experience of being interviewed in the open and closed question format. With this format, they reported they were able to consider areas of their experience to which they had previously never given much attention.

If the women knew of others who might be willing to be recruited into the sample, they were sent a written description of the research to give to the potential subject and asked to let the researcher know if that person desired to be contacted. This practice resulted in many subjects referring another and in the geographical sampling area being defined as the continental United States, as many subjects were referred from increasingly distant states.

Description of the Final Sample

The final sample for analysis of this dissertation consisted of thirty women who were selected according to the criteria put forth in the previous sections of this paper. Graphic descriptions of the final sample are displayed in Figures 2 through 15.

Demographic Data

Occupation at the Time of Conception

For purposes of this study, occupation was categorized by employment status (full- or part-time), student status, or full-time parenting. Subjects were asked to classify themselves by their primary occupation. Thirty-five percent of the subjects were employed at the time when their pregnancy was conceived. Twenty-three percent were college students, 19 percent were parenting, 15 percent were high school students, and 8 percent were unemployed. (Figure 2)

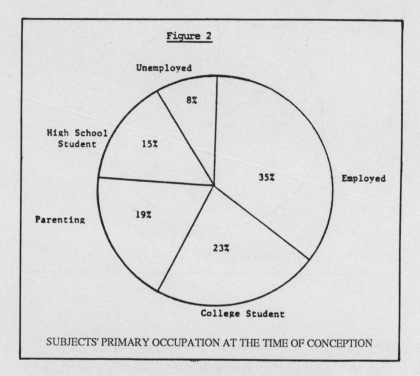

Figure 2

SUBJECTS' PRIMARY OCCUPATION AT THE TIME OF CONCEPTION

Educational Attainment at the Time of Abortion

Although 31 percent of the subjects had attained a Bachelor's degree in college at the time of the abortion, an equal number (31 percent) had attained only a portion of their high school education. Twenty-three percent of the subjects had attained some higher education, and 15 percent had obtained their high school diploma or GED. (Figure 3)

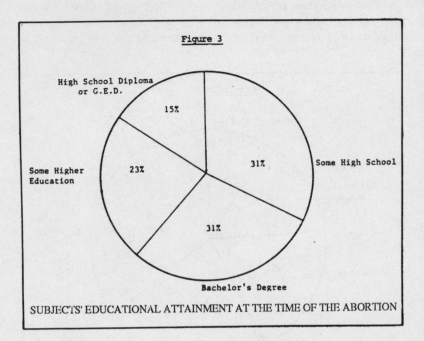

Figure 3

High School Diploma or G.E.D. — 15%

Some Higher Education — 23%

31% — Some High School

31% — Bachelor's Degree

SUBJECTS' EDUCATIONAL ATTAINMENT AT THE TIME OF THE ABORTION

Age When the Abortion was Performed

Age when the abortion was performed was self-reported, and in the case of multiple abortions, age at the first abortion was used. Thirty-one percent of the subjects were from 14 to 18 years of age at the time of the abortion. An equal number of subjects (31 percent) were ages 22 to 25. Twenty-three percent of the subjects were between 19 and 21, 7.5 percent were 26-30, and 7.5 percent were 31 to 36 years of age at the time of the abortion (Figure 4). There was no apparent difference, based on this variable, in terms of stress following abortion.

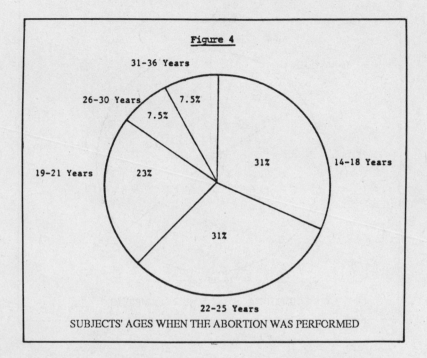

Figure 4

31-36 Years

26-30 Years

7.5%

7.5%

19-21 Years   23%

31%   14-18 Years

31%

22-25 Years

SUBJECTS' AGES WHEN THE ABORTION WAS PERFORMED

Subjects Age at the Time of Sampling

Subjects ages at the time of sampling ranged from 20 to 47 years of age, with the majority (36 percent) being between 31 and 35 years of age. Twenty-eight percent were between 26 and 30 years, 20 percent between 20 and 25 years, 12 percent between 36 and 40 years, and 4 percent between 41 and 47 years of age. (Figure 5)

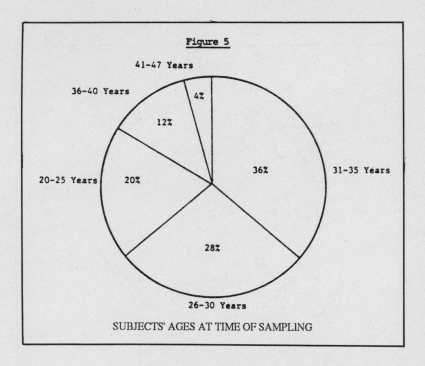

Figure 5

41-47 Years
36-40 Years
4%
12%
20-25 Years   20%   36%   31-35 Years
28%
26-30 Years

SUBJECTS' AGES AT TIME OF SAMPLING

Elapsed Period of Time Between the Most Recent Abortion and the Time of Sampling

The period of time that had elapsed between the subject's most recent abortion and the time of sampling ranged from one to twenty-five years, with the majority of cases being between five and ten years (64 percent). Twenty percent of the subjects had their abortions less than five years from the time of sampling; while for 8 percent, 11 to 15 years had elapsed; for 4 percent, 16 to 20 years had elapsed; and for 4 percent, 21 to 25 years had elapsed. (Figure 6)

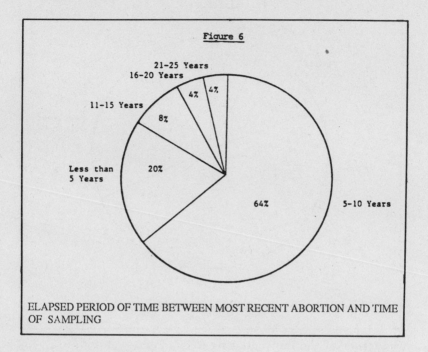

Figure 6

ELAPSED PERIOD OF TIME BETWEEN MOST RECENT ABORTION AND TIME OF SAMPLING

Race

All of the subjects in this sample were Caucasian.

Living Arrangements at the Time of Conception

Living arrangements at the time of conception were defined in terms of who the subject lived with during that period of time. Thirty-one percent of the subjects lived with their families of origin, while 27 percent lived with their impregnating partner. Twenty-three percent lived alone, 11.5 percent lived with one or more female roommate(s), and 7.5 percent had other living arrangements. (Figure 7)

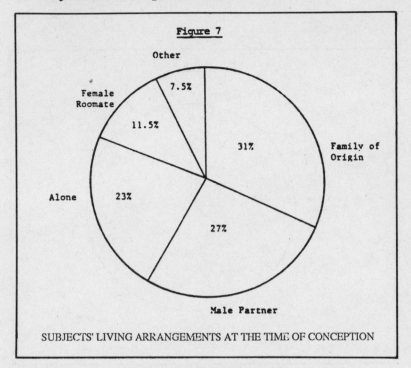

Figure 7

Other

7.5%

Female
Roomate

11.5%

31%   Family of
Origin

Alone   23%

27%

Male Partner

SUBJECTS' LIVING ARRANGEMENTS AT THE TIME OF CONCEPTION

Structure of the Impregnating Relationship

The structure of the relationship in which the pregnancy was conceived was categorized in terms of marital status, intent to marry, or other degrees of commitment to the future of the relationship. The majority of the relationships (45.5 percent) could be termed steady with commitments to the future. Of these, 30 percent were married, 50 percent were engaged or planning to be married, and 20 percent had informal commitments to the future. An additional 27 percent of the sample were in relationships termed "steady with no defined commitments to the future." Thus, the majority of women in the sample (72 percent) were in some sort of steady relationship at the time of conception. In addition to these, 18 percent of the pregnancies occurred in relationships with an estranged or ex-spouse. Half of these were pregnancies that occurred during a legal separation, and half as a result of resumed sexual relationship with the ex-spouse. The remaining 9 percent of the sample had pregnancies that resulted from a casual encounter. (Figure 8)

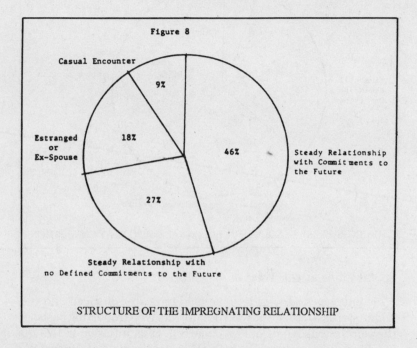

Figure 8

Casual Encounter — 9%

Estranged or Ex-Spouse — 18%

Steady Relationship with Commitments to the Future — 46%

27%

Steady Relationship with no Defined Commitments to the Future

STRUCTURE OF THE IMPREGNATING RELATIONSHIP

Primary Source of Financial Support at the Time of Conception

In addition to occupational data, subjects reported on the primary source of their financial support. Thirty-eight percent of the subjects were self supporting, while 27 percent were financially dependent on their parents, and 19 percent were dependent on their impregnating partner. Eleven percent were on some sort of welfare, and 4 percent reported other sources of support. (Figure 9)

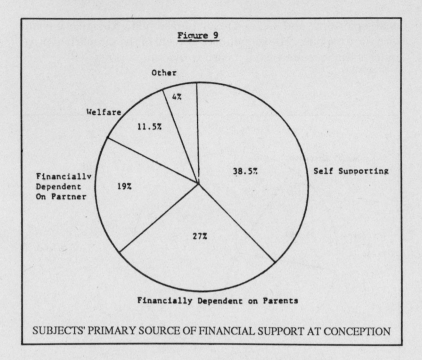

Figure 9

SUBJECTS' PRIMARY SOURCE OF FINANCIAL SUPPORT AT CONCEPTION

Social Class at the Time of Conception

Income was not considered a valid indicator of social and economic status for this study as the subjects were reporting based on the year in which conception occurred. High inflation in the '70s would make comparisions difficult. In addition, the subjects had widely disparate sources of financial support, making income comparisions even more difficult. Thus, it was felt that self categorization of socio-economic standing would be the most valid indicator of socio-economic status. Subjects were asked to self report socioeconomic status (i.e. lower, lower middle, middle, upper middle, upper class) based on their primary source of economic support.

Forty-six percent of the subjects classified themselves (at the time of conception) as middle class, 31 percent as lower class, 11 percent as lower middle class, 8 percent as upper middle class, and 4 percent as upper class. (Figure 10)

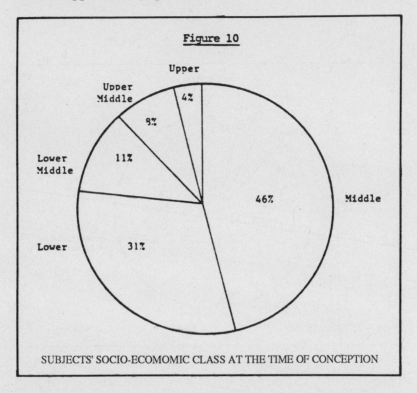

Figure 10

SUBJECTS' SOCIO-ECOMOMIC CLASS AT THE TIME OF CONCEPTION

Religious Beliefs

Subjects were asked to classify themselves in terms of religious beliefs as opposed to congregational affiliation. Reporting for the time period of the abortion, 72 percent reported having no specific religious beliefs that could be identified, 8 percent had beliefs represented by the Catholic faith, 8 percent had beliefs they classified as fundamentalist or born-again Christian, 4 percent classified their beliefs as Baptist, 4 percent as Presbyterian, and 4 percent as Jewish conservative. (Figure 11)

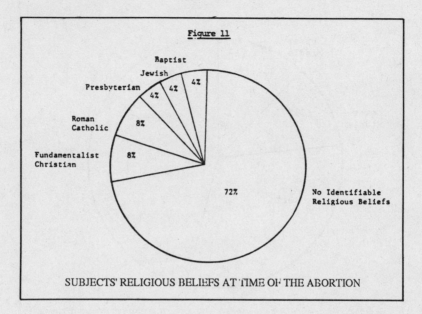

SUBJECTS' RELIGIOUS BELIEFS AT TIME OF THE ABORTION

Frequency of Abortions at the Time of Sampling

The majority of subjects (78 percent) had experienced only one abortion at the time of sampling, although 13 percent had experienced two, 4 percent three, and 4 percent four abortions in total. (Figure 12)

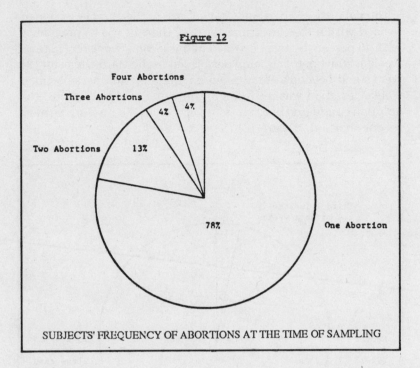

Figure 12

Four Abortions

Three Abortions

4%   4%

Two Abortions   13%

78%   One Abortion

SUBJECTS' FREQUENCY OF ABORTIONS AT THE TIME OF SAMPLING

Trimester in Which the Abortion was Performed

The trimester in which the abortion was performed was defined in two ways. For women who were informed by their doctors of the weeks gestation of their pregnancy at the time of the abortion this figure was used. For the remainder of the subjects recall was used to calculate weeks from conception to the time of the abortion. This unfortunately resulted in two systems of calculating elapsed period of gestation prior to the abortion, with the latter method resulting in an under-reporting of elapsed time by two weeks. This error in calculation could not be corrected as it was unclear to which subjects it applied. Nevertheless, under-reporting of weeks pregnant results in more conservative estimates which are to be preferred.

The majority of abortions (50 percent) in this sample were performed within the first trimester (less than 12 weeks pregnant), with 46 percent being performed in the second trimester (12 to 23 weeks), and 4 percent being performed in the third trimester (24 weeks and beyond). For women having had multiple abortions, weeks gestation was recorded for only one of the abortions: the abortion considered most stressful, or if equally stressful, the most recent abortion. (Figure 13)

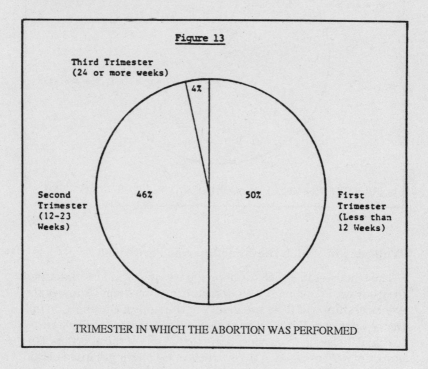

Figure 13

Third Trimester (24 or more weeks) — 4%

Second Trimester (12-23 Weeks) — 46%

First Trimester (Less than 12 Weeks) — 50%

TRIMESTER IN WHICH THE ABORTION WAS PERFORMED

Type of Abortion Procedure Performed

The majority of women in this sample (80 percent) had abortions performed by the most common methods: vacuum aspiration and dilation and curettage. While these two procedures are often used together, subjects were asked to specify whether vacuum aspiration as opposed to a D&C (possibly coupled with vacuum aspiration) was the procedure used. Sixty-five percent of the subjects had vacuum aspiration performed, 15 percent had dilation and curretage. Twelve percent of the subjects had their abortion induced by saline injection and 8 percent were aborted by dilation and evacuation procedures. (Figure 14)

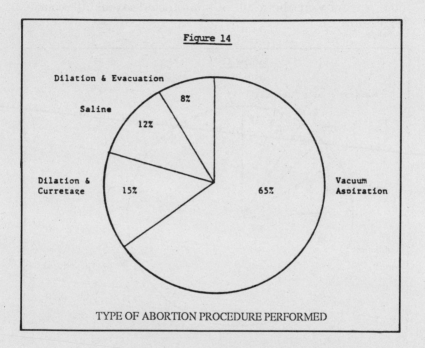

Figure 14

TYPE OF ABORTION PROCEDURE PERFORMED

Birth Control Practices Prior to Pregnancy

The majority of the sample (64 percent) reported using no birth control during the time when the pregnancy was conceived. Of those using birth control, few (8 percent) used the methods that are generally considered most effective (i.e. the pill or IUD). The most frequently mentioned methods of birth control were use of condoms (12 percent) and vaginal foam (8 percent), followed by use of the diaphram (4 percent), the IUD (4 percent), the pill (4 percent), and Natural Family Planning (4 percent). Although indicating the use of a contraceptive method, many of the women commented that its use was not regular nor conscientious. All of the pregnancies in the sample were classified by the subjects as unintended. Thirty-one percent were labelled contraceptive failures and sixty-nine percent were the result of unprotected sexual intercourse. (Figure 15)

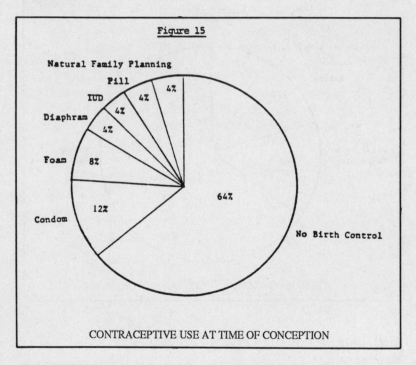

Figure 15

Natural Family Planning
Pill
IUD
Diaphram
Foam
Condom

4%
4%
4%
4%
8%
12%
64%
No Birth Control

CONTRACEPTIVE USE AT TIME OF CONCEPTION

Comparisons with National Norms

National data regarding abortion facilities, types of abortions, and the characteristics of women who obtain abortions are most comprehensively reported by the Alan Guttmacher Institute. Comparisions of this sample's characteristics with national norms collected by AGI resulted in a number of similarities regarding age, race, marital and parenting status, and incidence of previous abortions. As AGI reports, "In 1978, as in every year since 1973, the women who obtained abortions were mainly young, white, unmarried and childless; for most these were their first abortions" (Henshaw et. al 1981). This is also true for the present sample.

Age

National norms for age show that 15 to 24 year olds are the group among whom abortion utility is the greatest (Henshaw et. al, 1983). In 1978 about one third of all abortions were obtained by teenagers, one third by women aged 20 to 24; and one third, by women aged 25 and older (Henshaw et al, 1981). In the present sample 85 percent of the subjects obtained their abortions between the ages of 14 to 24 years. Forty-two percent were teenagers, 42 percent were aged 20 to 24, and 15 percent were women aged 25 and older. Thus it appears that although a slightly greater proportion of subjects in the present sample were younger at the time of their abortions, the overall age distribution is similar to national norms.

Marital Status

Seventy-five percent of abortions reported in 1978 were obtained by unmarried women (Henshaw et al, 1981). In this sample 77 percent of the subjects were unmarried at the time of their abortion.

Race

In 1978, 69 percent of all abortions were obtained by white women (Henshaw, et al, 1981). This sample contains only white subjects.

Previous Abortions

National norms for 1978, report 70 percent of aborters having experienced no previous abortions, as compared to 78 percent in the present sample (Henshaw et al, 1981).

Type of Abortion

Nationally, 95 percent of all reported abortions are performed either by vacuum aspiration or sharp curettage (includes the dilation and evacuation procedure) (Henshaw et al, 1981). In the present sample, 88 percent of the abortions were performed by these methods.

Trimester in Which the Abortion Is Performed

National norms show that in 1980, 91 percent of all reported abortions were performed within the first trimester of pregnancy (within 12 weeks since the last missed menstrual period) (Henshaw et al, 1983). In this sample, 69 percent of the abortions were performed in the first trimester. Thus in this sample a greater percentage of abortions (22 percent) were delayed into the second trimester. This difference may be partially accounted for by the increasing trend over the seventies for abortions to be performed in the first trimester (Henshaw et al, 1983).

Location Where Abortion Is Performed

1982 data report the majority of abortions occurred in clinics (56 percent), with 21 percent occurring in other nonhospital facilities, 5 percent in doctors' offices, and 18 percent in hospital settings (Henshaw et al, 1984). In the present sample 54 percent of abortions were performed in clinics, 8 percent in other nonhospital settings, 4 percent in doctors' offices, and 34 percent in hospital settings.

Summary of the Description of the Final Sample

Although the present sample was purposely selected to include only those women who had high stress abortion experiences, it is clear that demographically the present sample does not deviate significantly from national norms regarding abortion patients. Thus it is safe to assume that the high stress experiences of the subjects in the present sample are not linked to a demographic variable (or variables) that is not also present in a more nationally representative sample. Based on demographic comparisions only, the present sample appears to adequately represent national norms regarding abortion patients.

39

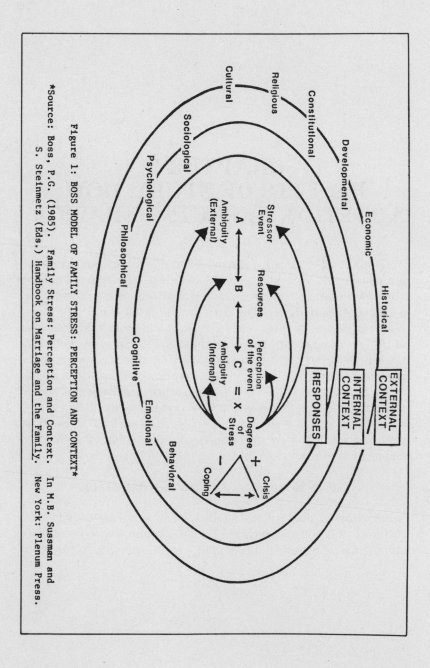

Figure 1: BOSS MODEL OF FAMILY STRESS: PERCEPTION AND CONTEXT*

*Source: Boss, P.G. (1985). Family Stress: Perception and Context. In M.B. Sussman and S. Steinmetz (Eds.) Handbook on Marriage and the Family. New York: Plenum Press.

CHAPTER 3
RESULTS OF STUDY: HOW
ABORTION EFFECTS BEHAVIOR

Although the focus of this research is essentially qualitative in nature, the interview schedule did include a series of fixed-choice questions relating to stress following abortion. (See Appendix for a listing of those items.) The data for the fixed-choice items are reported as a percentage of respondents who indicated presence of the stress indicator. Figures 16 through 29 display responses to these items. For reporting purposes, variables were grouped according to categories of stress following abortion that had been previously identified in the abortion literature. Indicators of stress following abortion that had not been previously identified in the abortion literature were grouped by the area of subjective experience to which they pertained (e.g., sexual function, fertility concerns, eating and weight maintenance, etc.).

Grief Reactions Following Abortion

Indicators of grief reactions following abortion are displayed in Figure 16 (following this section). The most commonly reported indicators of grief were feelings of grief, regret, sadness, sorrow, or a

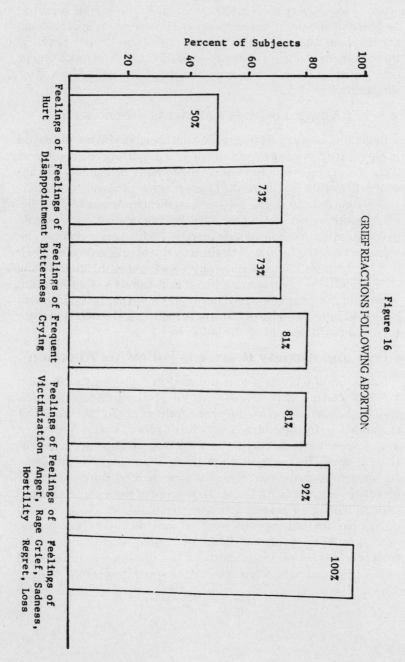

Figure 16

GRIEF REACTIONS FOLLOWING ABORTION

sense of loss. Every subject (100 percent) in the sample reported feeling one of more of these emotions. Frequent crying following the abortion was reported by 81 percent of the sample. Seventy-three percent of the subjects reported feelings of disappointment over the abortion, and 50 percent reported feelings of hurt after the abortion.

Angry Feelings Following Abortion

Indicators of angry feelings following the abortion are displayed in Figure 16 (following this section). A large portion of the subjects (92 percent) reported feelings of anger, rage, or hostility toward others following the abortion. These feelings of anger were alternately directed at self, one's partner, medical professionals, and significant others who were viewed as having taken a coercive role in the abortion decision making process. Eighty-one percent of the subjects reported feeling victimized by the abortion process. Feelings of victimization were generally associated with either feeling coerced into the abortion or a belief that significant information regarding the pregnancy resolution and abortion procedure had been withheld. Feelings of bitterness following the abortion were reported by 73 percent of the subjects.

Fear and Anxiety Reactions Following Abortion

Indicators of feelings of fear and anxiety following the abortion are displayed in Figure 17(following this section). Eighty-nine percent of the sample reported fear that others would find out about the abortion. In addition to fearing that others would find out, a large portion of the sample (58 percent) reported an increased distrust in men. This fear pertained mostly to men who were potential or actual sexual partners and to men who were doctors of obstetrics or gynecology. Fifty-four percent of the sample reported general feelings of anxiety following the abortion. These feelings did not pertain to any specific fear, but were diffuse feelings of fear, or anxiety. Fifty percent of the sample reported an increased distrust of others following the abortion. The others most often named (other than men who were categorized separately) were medical

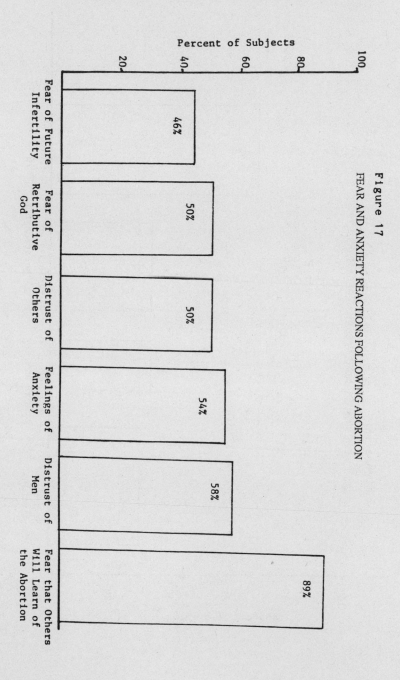

Figure 17

FEAR AND ANXIETY REACTIONS FOLLOWING ABORTION

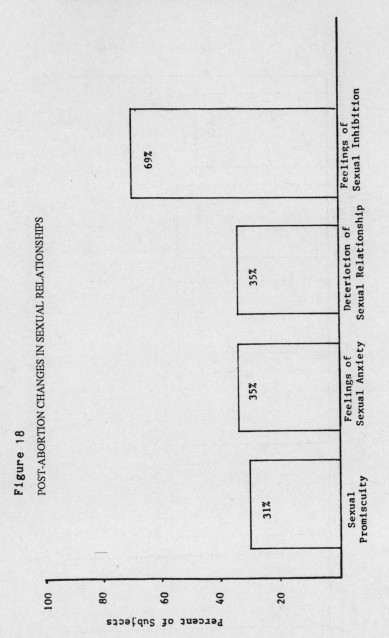

Figure 18

POST-ABORTION CHANGES IN SEXUAL RELATIONSHIPS

professionals: nurses and doctors in particular. These women indicated that they felt they had been lied to concerning the details of
abortion and many refused to visit a doctor for a lengthy period following the abortion, because they felt they could no longer trust
doctors.

Fifty percent of the sample reported feelings of fear concerning
punishment from God for having had the abortion. Fear of future
infertility was reported by 46 percent of the sample. This related
directly to the fear of punishment by God. Women fearing God's
punishment often reported that the punishment was expected in
the form of future infertility, i.e. that having had an abortion, they
would be denied the right to bear future children. Fears of infertility were caused by other factors as well. Little or no knowledge, as
well as increased knowledge of the abortion procedure, led many
of the women to question whether or not their reproductive organs
had been damaged. Future unsuccessful attempts to become pregnant, or miscarriage following the abortion were often linked in the
subjects' minds to their abortion experience, and infertility as a
result of the abortion was greatly feared.

Post Abortion Changes in Sexual Relationships

Post abortion changes in sexual relationships occurred for a large
portion of the subjects. These are displayed in Figure 18 (following
this section). Most frequently reported (69 percent) were feelings
of sexual inhibition following the abortion. Closely related to feelings of sexual inhibition were reports of increased feelings of sexual anxiety by 35 percent of the subjects. Feelings of sexual anxiety
and inhibition appeared to be linked to feelings of guilt and anxiety regarding the potential for another pregnancy. Although feelings of sexual anxiety were reported to cause a decrease in pleasure
in the sexual relationship, such feelings did not in all cases cause
sexual inhibition as well.

Sexual promiscuity following abortion was reported by 31 percent
of the subjects. Defined by subjects, sexual promiscuity was in most

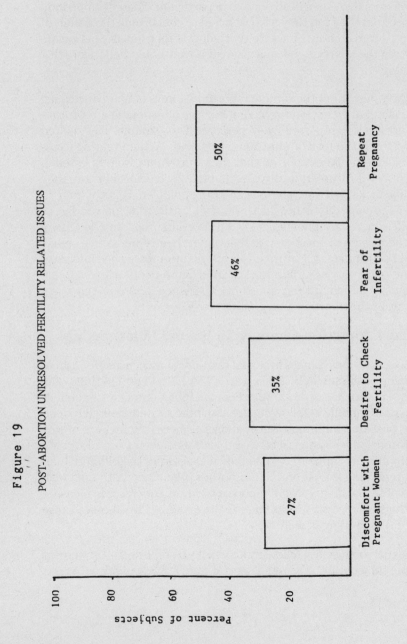

Figure 19

POST-ABORTION UNRESOLVED FERTILITY RELATED ISSUES

cases given the meaning of having many sexual partners, as opposed to one (or none) within a defined period of time.

In cases where the relationship continued past the abortion, 35 percent of the subjects reported a deterioration of the sexual relationship. This was often attributed to increased sexual anxiety and inhibitions which were related to guilt and fear of subsequent pregnancies. In many cases the relationships themselves were deteriorating, which contributed to and was augmented by the decreased pleasure in the sexual relationship.

Post-Abortion Unresolved Fertility Related Issues

Following the abortion, many of the subjects reported unresolved fertility issues. These are displayed in Figure 19 (following this section). Although abortion is generally thought to be evidence of not wanting to have a child at that particular time, 50 percent of the subjects reported a subsequent pregnancy carried to term within a short period of time following the abortion. Although pregnancies subsequent to abortion are not unusual, these pregnancies were self defined as being a repeat pregnancy related to the abortion. That is, the abortion experience was perceived by the subject as a catalyst for the subsequent pregnancy which was conceived shortly thereafter. Many of these subjects reported wanting to carry a subsequent pregnancy to term to make up for the aborted baby. For some this was couched in religious terms, for others it was simply a desire to have a child to make up for the loss experienced by the abortion.

Related to the issue of subsequent pregnancies was the fear of infertility following the abortion. Fear of future infertility was reported by 46 percent of the subjects. For some it was a religious issue, in that they believed that retribution for the abortion would come in the form of future infertility. Others based their fears of infertility on their knowledge of the risks associated with abortion, or on their perception of the abortion procedure as physically invasive and potentially damaging to their reproductive capacities. Fears of infertility were often augmented by a failure of the menses to return for an extended period of time, or by dramatic changes in

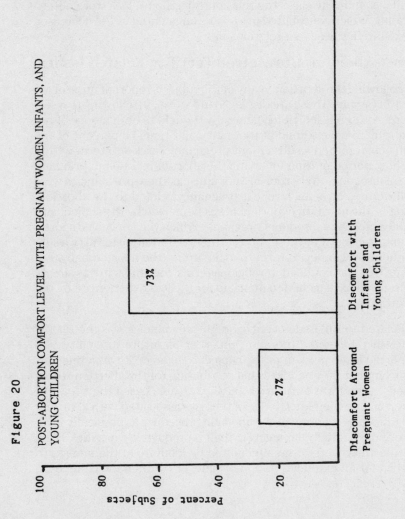

Figure 20

POST-ABORTION COMFORT LEVEL WITH PREGNANT WOMEN, INFANTS, AND YOUNG CHILDREN

the subject's usual menstrual cycle. Frustrated attempts to become pregnant subsequent to the abortion, or the occurrence of pregnancy complications such as miscarriage greatly contributed to fears of infertility. Women who did become pregnant subsequent to the abortion often reported a great deal of fear concerning the potential for pregnancy loss, complications, or fetal malformation caused by the previous experience of abortion.

Related to the fear of infertility, 35 percent of the subjects reported a desire to check their fertility. Although not all subjects reporting this desire acted on it, many did so.

Twenty-seven percent of the subjects reported discomfort with pregnant women. This was often discussed in terms of being a reminder of the abortion experience, and ambivalence over whether or not the abortion had been the right thing to do. Many women expressed feelings of guilt, remorse, jealously, and anger upon seeing another pregnant women.

Comfort Level with Pregnant Women, Infants, and Small Children

Following the abortion, many subjects reported intense levels of discomfort around other pregnant women, infants, and small children. These indicators are displayed in Figure 20 (following this section). The discomfort with pregnant women, reported by 27 percent of the subjects, seemed to relate to unresolved ambivalence over whether or not the abortion had been the right decision. Feelings of jealousy, a renewal of grief, sadness, and guilt were the feelings most often reported in conjunction with seeing other pregnant women. Invitations and attendance at baby showers were particularly difficult events for many of the subjects reporting this type of discomfort.

Discomfort with infants and small children following the abortion was reported by 73 percent of the sample. These reactions varied widely in intensity and content. On the one extreme, women reported feelings of grief, and jealousy when they came into con-

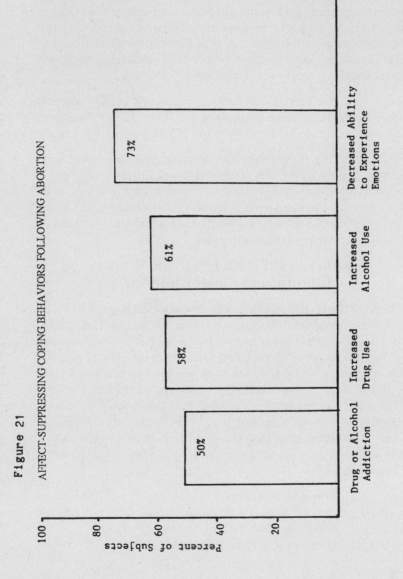

Figure 21

AFFECT-SUPPRESSING COPING BEHAVIORS FOLLOWING ABORTION

tact with an infant or small child. Others reported extreme guilt being triggered by the presence of children. One subject reported having high levels of hostility around infants, even to the point of feeling concerned enough to avoid contact with infants for fear of hurting them.

Affect Suppressing Coping Behaviors Following Abortion

Suppression of affect as a coping behavior was indicated by a large portion of the sample. Indicators of suppressed affect are displayed in Figure 21 (following this section). The most common affect suppressing behavior reported (73 percent) were direct reports of suppressed affect, or the inability to experience emotions (particularly painful emotions). This was reported most often in terms of emotional numbness or shock, although an inability to feel emotions, repression, and a shutting down of ones feelings were also used to label this reaction.

Affect suppression was also achieved through the increased use of drugs and alcohol. Sixty-one percent of the sample reported increased use of alcohol, and 58 percent reported increased use of drugs (both licit and illicit). Self reports of patterns of drug or alcohol addiction appearing to result from the increased dependence on drugs and alcohol following the abortion were reported by 50 percent of the subjects. Clearly many of the subjects had already developed an unhealthy reliance on drugs and alcohol use as a coping mechanism prior to the abortion, although many reported their first heavy use to have occurred in conjunction with the stress related to the abortion.

Post Abortion Changes in Eating Behaviors

Post abortion changes in eating behaviors, indicated by self report and changes in weight, are displayed in Figure 22 (following this section). Extremes of weight gain and loss were self-defined, as a ten pound weight loss for an underweight woman may be considered extreme, as for a heavier set woman, it may be considered desir-

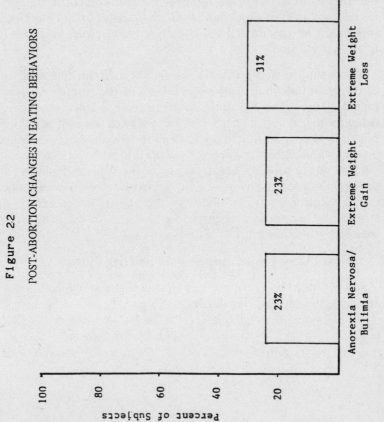

Figure 22

POST-ABORTION CHANGES IN EATING BEHAVIORS

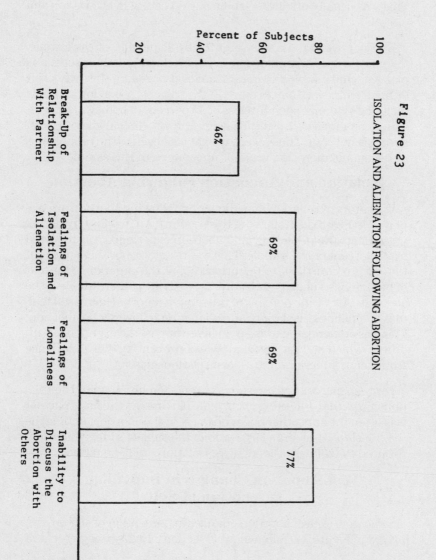

Figure 23

ISOLATION AND ALIENATION FOLLOWING ABORTION

able, with the opposite being true in the case of weight gain. Extreme weight gain was reported by 23 percent of the subjects. This was usually attributed to increased eating in efforts to calm oneself.

Extreme weight loss was reported by 31 percent of the sample. Twenty-three percent of the sample classified themselves as experiencing a period of anorexia nervosa. Again, this was a self defined malady, although many of the subjects reporting anorexia included evidence such as a loss of 25 percent of body weight, cessation of menses, hospitalization and/or clinical diagnosis of anorexia nervosa. Thus severe weight loss, even to the proportions of becoming anorectic, was not uncommon in this sample.

Isolation and Alienation Following Abortion

Indicators of isolation and alienation following abortion are displayed in Figure 23 (following this section). An inability to discuss with others the pregnancy and abortion experience was reported by 77 percent of the sample. This was usually reported in terms of finding it too difficult to tell others about the experience for fear of being judged negatively by others or having others disbelieve the account. Sixty-nine percent of the sample reported increased feelings of loneliness, isolation, and alienation following the abortion. This was often related to the inability to discuss the experience with others, which had the consequence of preventing that experience from being integrated into social relationships.

Forty-six percent of the subjects reported break-up of the relationship with the impregnating male partner. As the male partner was often the only other one who knew of the abortion, ending the relationship often left a large void in the subject's life, which contributed to feelings of loneliness, isolation, and alienation.

Post Abortion Changes in Individual's Perception of Self

Indicators of post abortion changes in perception of self are displayed in Figure 24 (following this section). Eighty-one percent of

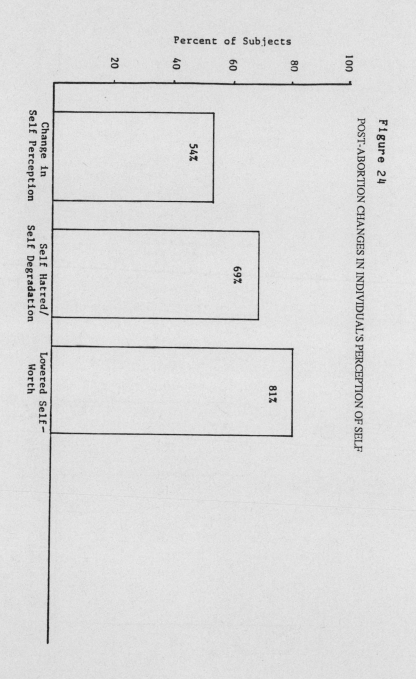

Percent of Subjects

Figure 24

POST-ABORTION CHANGES IN INDIVIDUAL'S PERCEPTION OF SELF

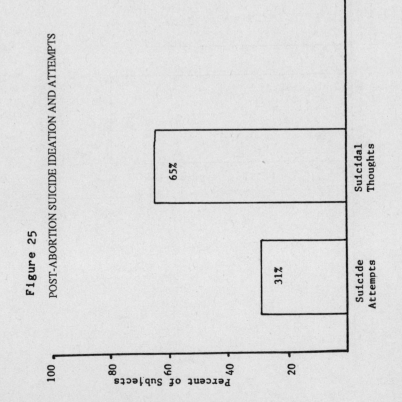

Figure 25

POST-ABORTION SUICIDE IDEATION AND ATTEMPTS

the subjects reported feelings of lowered self worth following the abortion. Sixty-nine percent reported feelings of self hatred and self degradation. These feelings were often linked to remorse and guilt associated with having had the abortion. Fifty-four percent of the sample reported a change in how self was perceived. This was often stated in terms of not recognizing ones self or of feeling a loss of identity.

Post Abortion Suicide Ideation and Attempts

Indicators of post abortion suicidal thoughts and actions are displayed in Figure 25 (following this section). Sixty-five percent of the subjects reported having suicidal thoughts as a reaction to the abortion experience, and 31 percent of the subjects made suicide attempts. Suicidal thoughts were generally reported in the form of having self destructive thoughts that were never translated into concrete actions. Contemplating driving off of the road, taking an overdose, wanting to die, etc., were examples given. Suicide attempts were in most cases drug and/or alcohol overdoses that resulted in being hospitalized.

Impaired Functioning Following Abortion

Indicators of impaired functioning subsequent to the abortion are displayed in Figure 26 (following this section). Feelings of depression were experienced by 92 percent of the subjects. Closely related to depression were reports of feelings of hopelessness (69 percent) and helplessness (69 percent). Inability to discuss the abortion experience with others and the perceived inabilty to gain access to the resources necessary to cope with the experience contributed to the feelings of depression, helplessness, and hopelessness. Sixty-one percent of the subjects reported increased feelings of nervous tension following the abortion, which related to reports of insomnia (42 percent) and decreased ability to concentrate (35 percent).

Pathological Responses of Significant Dysfunctional Nature

Indicators of pathological responses of significant dysfunctional nature following the abortion are displayed in Figure 27 (following

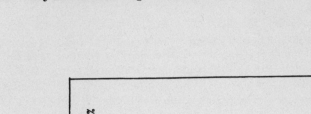

Figure 26
IMPAIRED FUNCTIONING FOLLOWING ABORTION

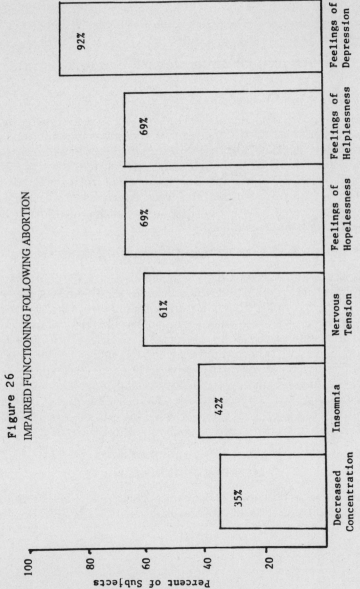

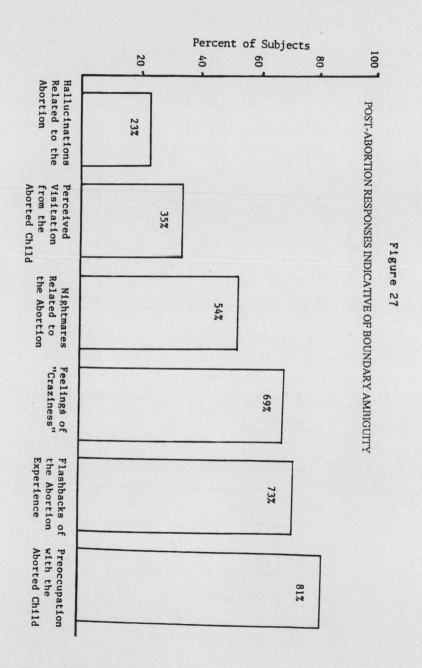

Percent of Subjects

POST-ABORTION RESPONSES INDICATIVE OF BOUNDARY AMBIGUITY

Figure 27

Hallucinations Related to the Abortion — 23%

Perceived Visitation from the Aborted Child — 35%

Nightmares Related to the Abortion — 54%

Feelings of "Craziness" — 69%

Flashbacks of the Abortion Experience — 73%

Preoccupation with the Aborted Child — 81%

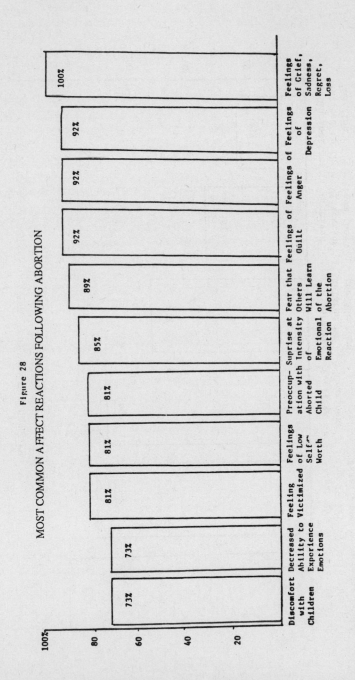

Figure 28

MOST COMMON AFFECT REACTIONS FOLLOWING ABORTION

this section). Although many of the coping strategies utilized in response to the stress caused by the abortion could be labeled dysfunctional, the following responses were particularly singled out, as they were of a nature that indicated a temporary, although significant departure from everyday psychological functioning.

Preoccupation with the characteristics of the aborted child was reported by 81 percent of the subjects. This preoccupation had many forms with the most common being thoughts centered around the dates the child would have been born and the age it would have attained at subsequent "birthdays." Wondering about the sex, eye and hair coloring, and stature of the child, had it been born, was also common. Just as expectant parents wonder whose genetic traits will be inherited, these subjects ruminated about what traits the child would have been endowed with. Anniversary dates, including most commonly the date of the abortion and the pregnancy due date, were time periods when preoccupation reached its peak. Preoccupation was also reported immediately following the abortion, particularly whenever another infant or small child was encountered.

Seventy-three percent of the subjects reported experiencing flashbacks of the abortion experience. Flashbacks were defined as reliving the experience in one's mind without making the clear distinction between experiencing a memory versus believing that the event was presently occurring. Subjects who had flashbacks of the experience generally reported very brief episodes of less than five minutes duration, although several had flashbacks lasting more than a couple of hours. The flashback experiences generally occurred in the evening as the subject was about to fall asleep.

Feeling "crazy" was reported by 69 percent of the subjects, with crazy being self defined. Most subjects defined feeling "crazy" as feelings of being "out of control" psychologically. Some had hallucinatory experiences that contributed to feeling "crazy" while others had no clear symptoms, but reported feeling near psychological collapse. Some subjects reported that they believed they experienced a nervous breakdown, although many of these did not seek psychological help, and thus such labelling was self diagnosis.

Fifty-four percent of the subjects reported having intense nightmares related to the abortion experience. Many of these consisted of graphic images of aborted fetuses that were in various states such as garbage heaps, pools of water, or activities such as trying to locate their mothers. The abortion experience was often relived in dreams. Guilt, remorse, and terror were associated with the nightmares.

While many of the nightmares consisted of being haunted by the aborted fetus, a portion of the sample (35 percent) reported actual feelings of being "haunted" by the aborted child. For some, this was a pleasant experience, such as a visitation from an aborted fetus that forgave its mother. For others it was a cause of great terror as the subject believed her aborted child was returning to condemn her.

Feelings of being haunted by the aborted child were often accompanied by visual, auditory, and tactile hallucinations. Twenty-three percent of the sample reported hallucinations related to the abortion. Some of these involved the aborted fetus, while others involved religious beings, such as angels, Christ, or souls of departed loved ones including the aborted child.

Most Common Affect Reactions Following Abortion

For purposes of comparision, the ten most commonly reported affect reactions (reported by 70 percent or more of the subjects in this sample) are displayed in Figure 28 (following this section). In order of predominance of reporting they are as follows: grief reactions (100 percent), feelings of depression (92 percent), feelings of anger (92 percent), feelings of guilt (92 percent), fear that others would learn of the pregnancy and abortion experience (89 percent), surprise at the intensity of the emotional reaction to the abortion (85 percent), feelings of lowered self worth (81 percent), feelings of victimization (81 percent), feelings of decreased affect, or suppressed ability to experience pain (73 percent) and feelings of discomfort around infants and small children (73 percent).

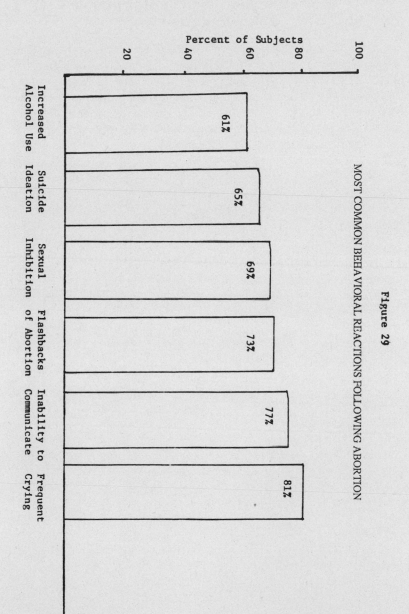

Figure 29

MOST COMMON BEHAVIORAL REACTIONS FOLLOWING ABORTION

Most Common Behavioral Reactions
Following Abortion

The most common behavioral reactions (reported by more than 60 percent of the subjects in this sample) are displayed in Figure 29. They are as follows: frequent crying (81 percent), inability to communicate with others concerning the pregnancy and abortion experience (77 percent), flashbacks of the abortion experience (73 percent), sexual inhibition (69 percent), suicide ideation (65 percent), and increased alcohol use (61 percent).

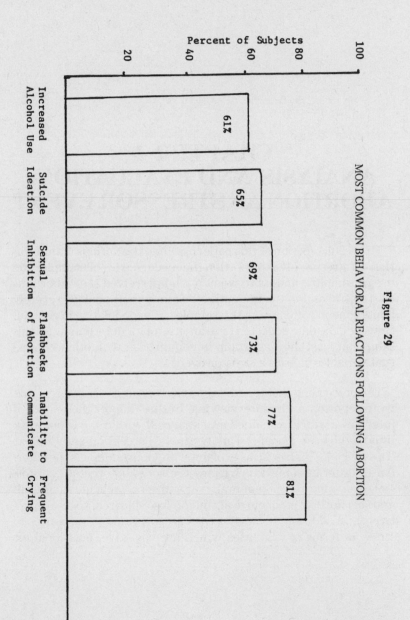

Figure 29

MOST COMMON BEHAVIORAL REACTIONS FOLLOWING ABORTION

CHAPTER 4
ANALYSIS AND EVALUATION: ABORTION AS STRESSOR EVENT

The results section of this paper outlined the various manifestations of stress related to abortion that occurred in this sample. The use of sampling limited to women who perceived their abortions as stressful and in the in-depth case study methodology severely limits generalizations from this sample to the population in general. However, the data collected here are useful for determining (in this sample at least) how abortion, in conjunction with other contextual variables, acts as a stressor event.

The preceeding chapter described twelve categories of stress that were reported in the interviewing. In this chapter the results of interviews will be examined and analyzed within the framework provided by the model of Family Stress: Perception and Context (Boss, 1985). This model, as explained previously, depicts the external and internal contexts in which a stressor event occurs (i.e. historical, economic, developmental, constitutional, religious, cultural; and sociological, psychological, and philosophical contexts, respectively). In addition, it clarifies the categorization of responses to stress in terms of responses which are cognitive, emotional, or behavioral. Using this model it is possible to examine a stressor event—the resources utilized to cope with it, the perceptions a subject has of the stressor event, and the subsequent degree of coping versus crisis—as a function of the contexts in which the stressor event occurs. (See Figure 1, p. 39)

Responses to Abortion As a Stressor Event

As a result of the interviews, it became clear that responses to abortion as a stressor event were not limited to one category of response but included cognitive, emotional, and behavioral responses.

Emotional responses to abortion as a stressor event were most dramatic, with grief, guilt, anger, fear, and depression being most predominant, with a large portion (over 85 percent) of the sample reporting experience with all five of these emotions.

Behavioral responses to abortion as a stressor event were widely varied, with the following responses being the most commonly reported: frequent crying, inability to communicate with others concerning the pregnancy and abortion experience, flashbacks of the abortion experience, sexual inhibition, suicide ideation, and increased alcohol use.

Cognitive responses were also varied in nature. A common cognitive response following the abortion was the motivation to learn more about pregnancy, fetal development, and abortion procedures. This learning appeared to be stress reducing in the long run, as it appeared to aid the subject in integrating the abortion experience into her perceptual and belief system. Initially, however, increased learning about pregnancy and abortion appeared to enhance stress. For many of the subjects, increased knowledge of fetal development and the methods by which the fetus was aborted caused a great deal of guilt, anger, and depression, which resulted in higher stress. For some subjects, it also caused a degree of concern (and anger) over what they had been told at the abortion facility concerning the fetus (i.e. that it was not a life, that it was a "blob," that it was "only a bunch of cells," etc.). Learning the risks of abortion also appeared to stimulate fears about future childbearing. In the long run, however, this increased learning seemed to enable an integration of the abortion experience with the subject's perceptual and belief systems.

Beliefs about abortion changed dramatically before and after the abortion experience. Reporting on their beliefs before the abortion, 38 percent believed abortion was wrong (11 percent of these labelling it "murder"), as opposed to 96 percent who believed it was wrong at the time of the interview. One may speculate that it was socially desirable for subjects, subsequent to their abortions, to report such a shift in beliefs regarding the morality of abortion. However, discussion of beliefs about the morality of abortion often revealed a time period during which a crisis and subsequent radical change regarding subjects' beliefs about abortion had occurred. This did not appear to be contrived.

The data concerning pre-abortion beliefs reveal that, although 35 percent of the subjects believed every woman ought to have the right to choose, an additional 27 percent had never really thought about abortion as a moral issue. Thus, in the time period after the abortion up to the time of the interview, these women had been confronted with abortion as a moral issue. Based on their cognitive response to their abortion experiences, which for many included increased learning about pregnancy and abortion, many had drastically altered their beliefs about the morality of abortion.

Other cognitive responses to abortion as a stressor event included a distrust of men (58 percent) and a distrust of others (50 percent). This occurred primarily in response to impregnating partners who the subjects often learned did not feel responsible for a pregnancy, and in response to medical professionals who the subjects often judged as less than honest.

All of the stress responses can be categorized within these three categories: emotional, cognitive, and behavioral. However, there is a great deal of overlap because emotions, thoughts, perceptions, beliefs, and behaviors often occur simultaneously and are often hard to separate from one another. Thus, for the purposes of this analysis, it was helpful to examine the stress responses in terms of the contexts in which they occurred and in relation to their use as potential coping mechanisms.

The Contextual Nature of Responses to Abortion as a Stressor Event

External Contexts

Historical Context

The historical context refers to the time period when the stressor event takes place (Boss, 1985). Over the last two decades dramatic changes have occurred in the manner in which abortions are obtained, performed, and perceived by the public. Liberalization of abortion laws in the early '70s (1973 Roe vs. Wade Supreme Court decision) changed the context of obtaining an abortion to one of demand, as opposed to limiting abortions to those women who were able to demonstrate that their pregnancies constituted a danger to their health or well-being. Although performance of illegal abortions continued to occur during the '70s and into the '80s, the majority of abortions nationwide during this time period were obtained legally. For this study, these changes in the historical context of abortion are explored in relation to the degree of post-abortion stress subjects experienced.

Legal versus Legitimate Abortion Procedures. Although all but one subject in this study obtained a legal abortion, many subjects made remarks questioning the legitimate nature of their abortion experience. The aspects of the abortion experience that were perceived by the subject as least legitimate were the manner in which informed consent procedures for the abortion were handled, particularly the pre-abortion counseling; the record-keeping concerning the abortion, especially regarding weeks gestation at the time of the abortion; and the actual and perceived need to travel long distances to obtain a confidential abortion.

Informed Consent Procedures. Informed consent procedures are a major part of any medical procedure. From a legal standpoint, the qualities that constitute informed consent include telling the patient "(1) the diagnosis, (2) the general nature of the contemplated procedure, (3) the risks involved, (4) the prospects of success, (5) the prognosis if the procedure is not performed, and (6) alternative methods of treatment, if any exist, as well as the relative risks and benefits of each of the alternatives" (American Jurisprudence Proof of Facts, 1976). Moreover, it is the physician's duty to pursue the requisite explanation of a procedure until it is clear that the patient understands.

The means by which informed consent for abortion was sought varied by the facility in which the abortions were performed. Subjects who received their abortions in physicians' offices generally were given a brief interview with the doctor or nurse, during which the abortion procedure was explained. Written literature and signed consent forms were not generally used. Clinic and hospital abortions, however, were more likely to require a signed consent form. Procedures in these facilities were rarely explained beforehand by the physicians performing them. Nurses or counselors were generally assigned the task of explaining the abortion procedures beforehand to subjects. Formal counseling sessions, held individually or in groups, preceeded the abortion procedure in many clinic facilities. However, in many cases, explanations were given after subjects had already signed the required consent forms and made payment for the abortion. In clinics and hospitals particularly, subjects remarked that one of the first things that they were asked to do was to pay for the abortion procedures in total. Oftentimes consent forms were also signed upon check-in, with the signature being required without explanations given nor time to read the printed form. In many cases signatures were required on the back of the consent form as payment was collected, which did not facilitate reading the form.

In the majority of cases where pre-abortion counseling was provided, it also followed payment and signature of consent forms.

Of those subjects receiving counseling prior to the abortion, 85 percent received it after making payment for the abortion. When questioned about whether or not they believed they could recover their money after the counseling session should they have decided not to proceed with the abortion, 65 percent said no and 15 percent were unsure.

The quality of explanations provided prior to the abortion was perceived by many subjects (92 percent) as inadequate. When asked to define what was inadequate about the explanations, subjects gave the following list of items:

1. Insufficient information about the specifics of the abortion procedure as applied to the subject's physical self (42 percent).

2. Insufficient information about the specifics of the abortion procedure as applied to the fetus or embryo (33 percent).

3. Insufficient or inaccurate information about the development of the fetus or embryo at the time of the abortion (67 percent).

4. Insufficient information pertaining to options regarding the abortion procedure itself and to the options of adoption or parenthood (37 percent).

5. Insufficient information regarding the medical risks and potential for psychological trauma following the abortion (29 percent).

Pre-abortion requests for more information, longer counseling, requests to speak with a more highly trained professional (i.e. a psychologist or social worker as opposed to the lesser-trained abortion counselors) or to speak with the physician prior to the abortion were denied to many subjects by abortion clinic personnel in particular. Clinics often maintained an orderly progression of subjects through stages of the abortion experience that would have been interrupted had such requests been granted.

Written materials were dispensed most often by clinics and hospitals as opposed to physicians' offices, although these were often dispensed following the abortion and related mainly to aftercare rather than information that would be helpful in making the abortion decision.

The fact that many subjects did not perceive the abortion service personnel as providing the opportunity for subjects to give their informed consent is evidenced by 32 percent of subjects stating that they felt the abortion personnel to some degree coerced them into the abortion by not giving them the information they needed to make an informed decision. Initially this may have been stress-reducing for many women as the lack of information appeared to enable them to have the abortion without having to confront their beliefs about abortion. After the abortion, however, when the panic concerning the unwanted pregnancy had diminished, many subjects expressed bitterness over having been given neither the opportunity nor the support to examine their feelings and beliefs concerning pregnancy and over not having been given all of the information they felt was necessary to have made an informed choice.

Many subjects took responsibility for this, stating that it would be too much to expect an abortion facility to outline clearly what an abortion involves in relation to the fetus and to future reproductive capacities. However, all of the subjects who were stressed by increased learning subsequent to the abortion expressed the wish that they had been informed of these things prior to the abortion.

Abortion Record Keeping. Many subjects were also aware of a deception taking place regarding the recording of weeks gestation at the time of the abortion. These subjects learned from the abortion personnel that the gestation of their pregnancies was to be recorded at an earlier stage of development in order to circumvent laws limiting the performance of abortion in that particular type facility or jurisdiction.

Subjects also reported their awareness that records were being filled out without reference to specific patients. Subjects learned this by watching clinic personnel record incorrect information on their charts, by the comments of personnel, and also by seeing records being filled out by clerks who appeared to be recording the same information for each file.

Subjects who obtained their abortions in a clinic or hospital often did not meet the doctor performing the procedure until it was about to commence, and, in many cases, the doctor was not introduced by name.

The inability to name the physician subsequent to the abortion, coupled with the knowledge that records were to some degree falsified, caused stress for many subjects who began to perceive the abortion personnel as less than trustworthy. It was also stress enhancing for those subjects who later wanted access to their abortion records.

Perceived or Actual Need to Travel. Although abortion became legal in every state after the 1973 Roe vs. Wade Supreme Court decision, many communities, particularly in rural areas, still do not offer abortion services due at least in part to lack of public acceptance of abortion. Many subjects in this study travelled out of their communities to obtain their abortions. Some travelled long distances to reach the nearest abortion facility, while others merely chose to go to the neighboring town to avoid being identified at the home-town-clinic.

Women who travelled out of a perceived need to preserve their anonymity, perceived their social world as hostile and unaccepting of abortion. For many subjects, travelling out of the community to obtain abortions precluded receiving abortion after-care from that particular facility. Although a post-abortion check-up and the necessary after-care could be performed by a woman's regular physician, many subjects who were concerned about maintaining their anonymity regarding the abortion, chose not to tell their doctors about the abortion. These subjects reported ignoring physical symptoms of distress following the abortion until the symptoms either subsided untreated or until seeking medical attention could no longer be delayed without risk to their lives. Those subjects whose symptoms could not be ignored often reported lying to their physicians about the abortion as a source of the symptoms, thus denying their physician a valuable piece of information necessary for treatment.

Fifty percent of the subjects reported travelling out of their communities to obtain their abortions. Subsequent to the abortion, 56 percent told their physicians about the abortion, while 44 percent kept it a secret. Sixty-one percent of the subjects in this sample had some sort of physical symptom following the abortion that in the subject's perception had been caused by the abortion. These symptoms ranged from heavy and prolonged bleeding to complications with subsequent pregnancies. Many went untreated.

The perceived need by many subjects for confidentiality regarding the abortion was stress enhancing in that it encouraged them to obtain the abortion outside of their own communities. Sharing the fact of the abortion with one's physician was often perceived by subjects to be more costly than potentially putting their health and future child-bearing capacities at risk. Thus, even in a historical context of legalized abortion, many of these subjects perceived abortion as having a high potential for causing social stigmatization.

These results clearly indicate that, although the historical context of abortion for these subjects included the legalization and institutionalization of abortion, moral legitimacy did not necessarily follow. Subjects continued to perceive abortion as a deviant act which in turn influenced the degree of stress they experienced.

One may speculate that for the subjects in the present study a majority of their socialization occurred prior to the '70s, during a time period when abortion was neither legalized nor highly accepted. This, coupled with having parents socialized in earlier decades, contributed to their perceptions of abortion as a socially stigmatizing event. Subjects born in the '70s and '80s and socialized by parents of another cohort may not perceive as great the need to hide their abortions for fear of social stigmatization, which in this sample was a contributor to certain manifestations of post-abortion stress. This is, of course, a question for further research.

Changes in the Diagnosis of Pregnancy. The development of new technology during the last decade regarding pregnancy testing has marked the historical context of abortion decision-making also. Few women in this sample had access to home pregnancy tests at the time of their pregnancies. However, blood tests had replaced urine tests for many subjects, allowing for earlier diagnosis of pregnancy. Pregnancy diagnosis in the first trimester allowed many of the subjects to make their abortion decisions before the second trimester had begun. The effects of such technology on stress related to abortion is important since delays in pregnancy diagnosis mean the woman had a more developed pregnancy at the time she was making her decision and at the time of the abortion. Based on subject reports, increased fetal development at the time of pregnancy diagnosis appeared in this sample to contribute to post-abortion stress in terms of guilt and grief over aborting a more developed fetus and in terms of the increased physical involvement with the fetus that a woman may have experienced in a more developed pregnancy and abortion.

Changes in Abortion Technology. Abortion technology has also changed over the last decade. The most significant changes include the shift to increased use of vacuum aspiration procedures in early pregnancy and the use of dilation and evacuation procedures in later pregnancy. Saline and prostaglandin induced abortions were used routinely in the early and mid-'70s to abort later-term pregnancies. Abortions by saline or prostaglandin induction require the patient to go through a period of labor and delivery of the aborted fetus, with the possibility, in prostaglandin abortions, of the fetus sometimes surviving the procedure. Such abortions in later pregnancy are now largely being replaced by the use of dilation and evacuation procedures which are thought to be less traumatic to abortion patients because the latter do not require the patient to undergo the labor and delivery phases necessitated by a saline and prostaglandin induced abortion. Increased use of vacuum aspiration abortions is also believed to decrease the stress related to abortion, as it is less likely to cause the complications (i.e. perforated uteruses and other unintended puncture wounds) of the dilation and curettage procedure that it has largely replaced (Henshaw, et al, 1982).

The majority of subjects in this sample obtained vacuum aspiration abortions. However, later-term abortions in this sample were primarily performed by saline induction as opposed to the dilation and evacuation procedures. Although stress in this sample was experienced in conjunction with a representation of each of the abortion techniques, based on subject reports it was apparent that certain manifestations of stress were enhanced by the physical aspects of each of the abortion procedures. Saline abortions were perhaps the most pronounced in this regard.

Saline Abortions. It was apparent that all of the subjects undergoing saline abortions were highly stressed by the physical process of labor and delivery inherent in this type of abortion. The labor was prolonged and painful. Subjects reported experiencing a great deal of remorse and recrimination as they went through the process of aborting a fetus that was premature but fully formed. Those who saw their aborted fetuses were shocked by the burns caused by the saline and by the horror of seeing a fully formed fetus that looked like a small baby. All of the women having saline induced abortions were bitter about the lack of preparation they received regarding the abortion procedure. None felt that they had been adequately informed regarding the length and degree of labor pains that would be experienced, or the physical development that the fetus would have attained if they saw it, or the burns and scarring that the fetus would have sustained from the saline.

In particular, all of the saline abortion subjects mentioned the stress and immediate remorse that occurred during the induction of the saline, at which time the fetus, which may or may not have quickened prior to this time, began an apparent struggle for life. Violent kicking and punching on the part of the fetus as its amniotic fluid was filled with the caustic saline solution was psychologically unbearable to the subjects, who stated that they were totally unprepared for such an event. The urge on the part of some subjects to protect the fetus as it struggled for life by requesting that the abortion be stopped at once, was reportedly met with terse replies by nurses who stated that a saline induction is irreversible. Thus, unprepared subjects reported enduring an hour of labor to deliver a fully formed fetus. These subjects had been totally unprepared for such an experience, as the following remarks illustrate:

"I guess most of the women didn't realize what it was you had to go through. You're really not educated at all. And I know if I had been educated I would never have made the choice to do it. So I went into really hard labor, and it's so much pain; I've never experienced such pain in my whole life as that had been. You know I've had a baby since then, but it was really, it was such intense pain that if I had had something in my room to kill me, I would have, to get myself out of the misery."

"The doctor just said, 'You'll have some mild cramps, expel the fetus, then it will be all over.' And it wasn't mild cramps, expel the fetus, and it will be all over . . ."

" . . . And the minute the salt goes in, the baby goes into convulsions, inside you can feel it flopping around in there, just fighting for life."

"And I guess within an hour after everyone got finished in the treatment room . . . the whole ward . . . I don't know how the nurses stood it . . . I would have had a nervous breakdown. The whole ward . . . the women were screaming and crying to keep their babies. And it was like they were screaming for mercy and saying like, 'Oh God, please help me' and 'God, forgive me' and they were just screaming out, and they were saying, 'I am sorry' and things like, 'I want my baby'."

Vacuum Aspiration Abortions. Vacuum aspirtion abortions also appeared to contribute to subsequent stress in a manner unique to the procedure. Subjects obtaining vacuum aspiration abortions uniformly reported that the painfulness of the procedure was much more intense than the prior explanations had prepared them for. Concerns following the vacuum aspiration procedure related mainly to future reproductive capacities and to the experience of the fetus or embryo. A lack of understanding of how the procedure worked (i.e. only the uterus is suctioned) caused many subjects to perceive the procedure as destructive to their reproductive organs. They feared that the high-powered suction had removed more than just the fetus. Dilation of the cervix by mechanical means became a stressor for subjects who subsequently became concerned over whether or not their cervixes had been damaged. This concern was enhanced for subjects who miscarried later pregnancies or were subsequently diagnosed with cervical incompetence (an inability of the cervix to withstand the weight of a developing pregnancy).

Subjects also expressed concern over the pain that may have been experienced by the fetus or embryo as it was expelled by the suction procedure. Many subjects remarked that as the suction procedure commenced they experienced a sudden subjective change in their physical experience of self which they attributed to the ending of the pregnancy and death of the fetus or embryo. Although this physical sensation may be attributed to the hormonal change that would begin as the pregnancy was terminated, these subjects perceived it as an indicator that a death had occurred, which appeared to be a highly stress-enhancing perception. All of these concerns engendered a range of feelings including guilt, grief, fear, anger, and depression.

Vacuum aspiration patients were the most likely to report an inability to experience emotions following the abortion. This appeared to be linked to the intense painfulness of the procedure, coupled with the highly charged emotional reactions to it, which were compressed into a relatively short time period that did not appear to allow the subjects to process the emotional content of the experience adequately until much later. Relieved to be rid of the pain, many subjects reported closing off their emotions from conscious examination in an effort to recover from the experience. This appeared to be a viable short-term coping mechanism which enabled the women to recover immediately from the procedure. However, when continued, it subsequently contributed to a sense of alienation and isolation from others.

Dilation and Curettage Abortions. For most subjects in this sample the dilation and curettage procedures were performed under anesthesia. The use of anesthesia appeared to contribute to reduced stress because, unlike the other procedures, the women did not have intense physical experiences that became emotionally charged. The few subjects who obtained dilation and curettage abortions without anesthesia reported that it was a highly painful experience. Concerns subsequent to these types of abortions were similar to the vacuum aspiration procedures (i.e. concern over potential damage to reproductive capacities and concern over the experience of pain by the fetus or embryo).

Dilation and Evacuation Abortions. Subjects who obtained dilation and evacuation abortions generally had a two-day procedure performed, beginning on the first day with cervical insertion of a laminaria wick to dilate the cervix, and followed on the second day by the removal of the fetus. These abortions were generally performed under anesthesia. Stress appeared to be generated by the insertion of the laminaria wick (used to dilate the cervix) which began an irreversible procedure. Second thoughts during the waiting period prior to the fetal evacuation were common. A counterbalance to this, however, was the reassurance many women later had that their cervixes had been gently dilated over a 24-hour time period which was less likely to cause harm than other types of dilation. Concerns subsequent to this type of abortion were mainly focused on the pain that the fetus may have experienced and guilt over the knowledge that a second or third trimester fetus had been dismembered in this manner.

Abortion by Hysterotomy. Only two subjects received abortion by hysterotomy and these were not their first abortions. In both cases they proved highly stressful. Abortion by hysterotomy is similar to a Caesarian section delivery of a second or third trimester pregnancy, the difference being that the intent is to deliver a dead versus a live fetus. Interuterine strangulation is used, in most cases, to insure an abortion versus live birth. Concerns with this type of abortion were focused on the experience of the fetus. Guilt and grief were experienced by both subjects. One subject in particular was guilt-ridden and angry when she learned from the attending nurse that her twins, aborted by hysterotomy, had been born alive but allowed to bleed to death when the doctor neglected to tie their umbilical cords.

Cultural Context

The cultural context in regard to abortion has a great deal of overlap with the historical and religious contexts. Thus, it will only be discussed briefly, with further discussion found under these other headings. The cultural context of families is defined by Boss (1985) as "that which provides the canons and mores by which families define events of stress and their coping resources." Although this research confined itself to the individual's perceptions of the abortion experience, the researchers did gain a great deal of insight into how the individual viewed her family and social systems regarding the abortion event.

It became apparent in this sample that abortion was not a socially acceptable event in many of the subjects' social systems, and thus was omitted from discussion. Family-of-origin and religious systems in particular were viewed by the subjects as unaccepting of the abortion experience often because of a set of family or religious rules that defined out-of-wedlock sexual intercourse by members of the family-of-origin as unacceptable behavior not fit for family discussion.

Reiss (1981) defines the totality of family beliefs, which would include their beliefs regarding sexuality, as the "family paradigm." Family paradigm is a helpful concept for understanding families where out-of-wedlock sexuality is perceived as a violation of the family belief system. Family paradigm is defined by Reiss (1981) as the fundamental and enduring assumptions about the world that family members share and have developed over the course of the family's history together. These assumptions are shared by all family members, despite disagreements that exist within the family. Most importantly, the core of an individual's membership in his or her own family is the acceptance of, belief in, and creative elaboration of these beliefs.

Thus, for subjects who become pregnant in families that have beliefs opposing out-of-wedlock sex, the decision of whether or not to abort includes contemplating whether or not the family can survive a challenge to its paradigm should the pregnancy (and antecedent sexual behaviors) be revealed. In this sample it appeared that individuals often made the decision to abort as a means of protecting the family paradigm from stress and thus protecting their membership in the family-of-origin. This was often at the cost of increased personal stress.

Many subjects in this study clearly perceived their sexual behaviors leading to pregnancy and their abortion experience as behaviors that, if admitted into the family's conscious awareness by discussion, may have caused either a family crisis or expulsion from the extended family, as the following remarks indicate:

> "They'd kill me (speaking of her parents). I thought I'd rather kill myself."

> "There is something about telling your parents about out-of-wedlock sex . . . protecting them from sex."

> " . . . My mother was a very strict person . . . I didn't think she would receive it very well, which was my mistake, because in fact later, after I had the abortion, I

started hemorrhaging and I had to tell her because I had
to have someone to take care of my daughter . . . You
think that your parents are going to kill you, but apparently they won't.''

The family paradigm operating in these extended families
included beliefs that did not allow for the discussion of out-of-
wedlock sexual activities and thus subjects perceived members of
their extended family as being unavailable to help with the pregnancy resolution. The need to keep the abortion a secret, at least
within the extended family appeared to cause alienation from the
family as emotional needs could not be admitted nor addressed.
Moreover, the need for secrecy severely limited obtaining coping
resources from both within and outside of the family system. Anyone who might reveal the secret of the pregnancy or abortion to
family members was discarded as a potential source of help, and
confidentiality was often preserved at great personal costs.

As with most family secrets, the sexual behaviors leading to the
pregnancy and the abortion were often known of by extended
family members, but a collusion occurred to keep the knowledge
of the "secret" a secret. Thus, many subjects never told their parents about the abortion (40 percent), but remarked that they were
quite sure that their parents knew of it or at least suspected it.

Social acceptance of abortion in other primary systems was also
limited for many subjects. Many subjects consulted friends and
acquaintances for advice prior to the abortion. Acquaintances were
often selected based on their prior abortion experiences. The subjects often learned from acquaintances where to obtain an abortion and other details relating to it, but did not receive much in the
way of social support relating to the emotional aspects of the pregnancy and abortion experience.

However, subjects reported receiving a great deal of emotional
support from friends prior to the abortion. Emotional reactions to
the pregnancy were discussed in detail with friends, with friends

being the most likely consultants to advise abortion. Emotional reactions to the abortion, however, were less acceptable topics of discussion. Many subjects reported that friends who had been enthusiastic supporters of the abortion decision were unwilling to listen to any accounts of the stress produced by the abortion. It appeared that the norm with friends was to repress or deny any stress that may have occurred as a result of the abortion. This appeared to be a protective strategy on the part of friendship systems to avoid having to deal with the pain of abortion. Thus, the friendship system, like the family system, avoided stress by containing it within the individual. This appeared to lead to feelings on the part of subjects, of alienation and isolation, along with self-doubt and recriminations for feeling stress. Upon learning that their emotional reactions to the abortion were unacceptable topics of discussion among friends, many subjects questioned the validity of their emotional reactions. This self-doubt appeared to contribute to increased stress and the use of coping through denial and repression.

The stress of abortion was relieved for many subjects only after they found social systems that allowed them to express their feelings concerning the abortion. Surprisingly, for many subjects this outlet was found among pro-life and fundamental religious groups. In these social systems subjects found members who allowed them to discuss freely their feelings of grief, guilt, loneliness, anger, and despair. They also found that members of these systems were not adverse to discussing the details of the abortion experience, particularly with reference to concerns over pain that the fetus may have experienced and damage that may have occurred to the subjects' reproductive organs. In other social systems these concerns had not been validated.

Coping with the abortion experience by discussing it with members of groups whose beliefs concerning abortion were conservative (i.e. either in terms of religious fundamentalism or having pro-life views), appeared to have a marked influence on the subjects' own beliefs concerning the abortion. Those that found relief in religious groups increasingly began to perceive the abortion as the taking of a life. Thus the abortion was defined as a "sinful" event that needed to be repented. This came in terms of confessing it to "God" and receiving forgiveness. The subjects who affiliated themselves with members of pro-life groups also increasingly viewed abortion as the taking of a life. They became increasingly angry about the way abortion had been explained to them by their health care providers and angry over the manner in which their abortions were performed. Many learned a great deal from pro-life groups about fetal development which initially increased their guilt, grief, and anger. Since the pro-life groups also had religious components that included Christian beliefs, the subjects who were influenced in this manner also dealt with their abortions by perceiving it as a sin that required repentance. Anger towards others was dealt with by perceiving the need to forgive these others.

Many subjects reported a change in their beliefs concerning abortion, from viewing it as a matter of free choice prior to their abortion (35 percent), to viewing it as the taking of a life or as murder (96 percent) subsequent to their abortion. One could speculate that beliefs altered in this manner would be in opposition to efforts to cope with the abortion, but this was not the case for many subjects. Positive coping (leading to decreased subjective experiencing of stress) appeared to occur for many subjects when they became affiliated with friends whose belief systems defined abortion as the taking of a life. Initially, coping occurred by being able to talk to such friends about the abortion experience and having them accept it, albeit with a judgmental bias of viewing abortion as "sinful." The judgmental component inherent in such friendships was initially stress-enhancing. It appeared to increase, or at least increase awareness of, feelings of grief and guilt. This stress was alleviated, however, by the accompanying beliefs of this social system that allowed for repentance and forgiveness. Thus, a subject could avoid the judgment component by repenting of her "sin" and this led to her increased acceptance within the social system.

It was an unexpected result that joining a social system with conservative religious beliefs regarding abortion would serve as a coping mechanism for many subjects. Further research is obviously needed to understand how the belief systems of the social system to which a subject belongs, or with which she becomes affiliated, serve to increase or decrease the stress of abortion. This study has highlighted it as an area contributing to stress that needs further examination.

Religious Context

The religious context of the family refers to the religious beliefs of the family members as well as the beliefs of the religious body or social group that the family members have as their religious reference group (Boss, 1985). Religious beliefs concerning sexuality, pregnancy, and the abortion experience were explored to learn how they related to abortion as a stressor.

As the preceeding section stated, religious beliefs concerning sexuality and abortion, filtered through the various social systems with which the subjects were affiliated (i.e. family, friends, etc.), appeared to have an influence over the degree of stress experienced and the various means of coping.

Religious beliefs had a great deal of influence over how sexuality was viewed. Many of the subjects either held religious beliefs, or came from families that held religious beliefs, that defined out-of-wedlock sexual intercourse as ''sinful.'' In both cases such beliefs caused a great deal of stress when sexual behaviors were not congruent with beliefs. The dominant manner of coping with such stress in this sample was through the use of the defense mechanisms of repression and denial, as the following quotes illustrate:

> ''I was fully aware of the fact that if you sleep with somebody there is the possibility of pregnancy and you've got to be prepared for that. But you really do believe that you are not going to be the one. I guess there always was that possibility to worry about in the back of my mind, and it would crop up at that time when it was the end of the month cycle . . . I was slightly aware, 'Is this going

to work out right or something?' But that is something
that you can really just divorce yourself from . . . you
push it out of your mind."

"You always think it won't happen to me. I had been sexually active since I was 18 and had not gotten pregnant.
Even though I had been on birth control pills on and
off . . . you always think, oh it won't happen to me."

"You kind of do this thing in your mind and tell yourself,
'Oh, not me . . . I couldn't be pregnant.' So you kind of
push it back in your mind and you know. When I found
out I was pregnant, I was three months along. And that
kind of knocked me over."

Repression and denial were used both on a personal and systems
level. In the cases where subjects' beliefs concerning sexuality were
incongruent with their actions, the subjects repressed or denied
their sexual behaviors to themselves, often to the point of including denial of the need for effective contraceptive practices. In the
cases where only the family beliefs were incongruent with the sexual behaviors of the subject, the subject and her family colluded
to keep the sexual activity a secret. Thus, although both the subject and her family often knew that sexual activity was occurring,
this was a taboo subject that was never raised for fear of upsetting
delicate family relationships. The family paradigm (Reiss, 1981) in
this regard was thus one of denial and repression on a systems level.

Although repression and denial were highly effective coping
mechanisms for resolving the stress caused by the incongruity
between beliefs and behaviors, these coping mechanisms contributed to a higher level of stress at the time of the abortion. Abortion was often resorted to in this sample as a means of continuing
the repression and denial behaviors, which was often at great personal cost. Subjects who had a desire to keep their child believed
that it would be too costly to the family paradigm concerning sexuality, and thus abortion was the only perceived alternative to

destroying the family-of-origin belief system. This was often a trade-off of high personal stress in favor of low stress to the family system.

In addition, the need for secrecy concerning the pregnancy and abortion robbed the subject of her family members as potential sources of emotional support during a difficult decision phase and during the experience of the abortion and its aftermath. Many subjects reported a high degree of alienation and isolation from their family members as a result of the need to protect the family belief system, as the following quote illustrates:

> "Oh the anxiety [of keeping the abortion a secret] was tough. Then when you know it's the worst crime to have taken your child's life because the family you come from scorns that more than the pregnancy. I was really concerned about that. But at the same time I desperately wanted somebody to find out . . . somebody who loved me. That was a mixed bag."

Subjects who belonged to social systems who viewed an out-of-wedlock pregnancy as unacceptable, also were often confronted with beliefs that defined abortion as equally unacceptable. Thus, a conflict arose for these subjects from the need to decide which beliefs were more costly to violate. Since violating the religious prohibition against abortion could occur in relative secrecy, whereas carrying the pregnancy to term involved outwardly defying the family-of-origin's religious belief system, abortion was often viewed as the least costly of the two choices. As mentioned in preceeding sections, this decision-making regarding beliefs often involved the perceived need to preserve one's membership in the family system by not openly challenging the family's beliefs regarding out-of-wedlock sexuality. This decreased the potential stress to the system, perhaps at a cost of greater stress to the subject who had the burden of maintaining her secret through a time when her family resources may have been helpful. Thus, religious beliefs often prevented a subject from requesting aid from her family in the difficult decision-making phase regarding pregnancy resolution and the subsequent experience of abortion. This inability to ask the family for help in coping with the pregnancy was later regretted by some subjects who later felt their family would have survived the crisis in beliefs and gone on to be very supportive. This was an especially difficult realization for women who stated that their main reason for aborting was to preserve the family homeostasis. In either case, keeping the pregnancy and abortion a secret in an effort to preserve the family belief system often appeared to alienate and isolate the subject from her extended family system. This, in turn, contributed to her experience of stress, as the following quote illustrates:

> "I would have appreciated being able to go to my parents as they always offered . . . I would have enjoyed being able to have their support, being able to know it (carrying the baby to term) was the right thing. I knew they already said it was . . . It wasn't that they didn't want me to come to them. It was a concept in our society with saying, 'Don't tell them, you'll hurt them. Don't tell them, you'll embarrass them.' Almost so that I had forgotten that they had told me themselves (that she could come to them for help) and I believed what was a pervasive idea."

Religious beliefs were also important regarding coping with the guilt and grief caused by abortion. Subjects who had intense and conflicting emotions about the abortion often turned to religious friends, acquaintances, or to their perception of God. In each case, the other was selected as someone who would validate the need for guilt and grief with the belief that a human life had been taken, and that forgiveness was available for this "sin." Relief came from repentance for the "sin" of abortion and the belief in a forgiving versus a retributive God.

It became apparent that many subjects initially held a religious belief in a retributive God. Such a perception led to a great deal of fear and anxiety, as it was not uncommon for these subjects to report a fear that God would punish them for the abortion by denying them future fertility. Such beliefs causing high stress could only be resolved by either working within the belief system to find forgiveness or rejecting the belief system entirely. In most cases both strategies were used with the final result being an acceptance of the original beliefs with a greatly modified view of God as a forgiving versus a retributive power. Interestingly, this resolution often occurred in the context of future childbearing, with the subsequent child perceived as an outward sign of God's forgiveness of the subject's past actions.

Developmental Context

The developmental context refers to the state in the life cycle of both individuals and the family itself (Boss, 1985). The developmental context of the subject was explored with particular reference to her previous and subsequent childbearing history and her relationship to her family-of-origin and her impregnating partner.

For most subjects, the aborted pregnancy was their first pregnancy. Fifty percent of the subjects had experienced subsequent pregnancies at the time of sampling. Of the remainder, the majority were planning or wished to bear children in the future. A small portion of the sample were women who had experienced pregnancies carried to term previous to the abortion. Of these, many experienced subsequent childbearing after the abortion as well. Thus, for the majority of subjects, the abortion was an event that was in response to an ill-timed pregnancy as opposed to a lack of intent to ever bear children.

This is an important consideration in terms of stress related to the abortion, because for women intending to carry a subsequent pregnancy to term, the abortion must be viewed in relation to its impact on issues regarding future fertility.

Many of the subjects (73 percent) reported coping with their emotional reactions to the abortion by the use of suppressed affect, or the inability to experience emotions (particularly painful emotions) after the abortion. For many subjects the suppressed affect coping strategy went uninterrupted until future fertility issues were confronted. At such times a great emotional outburst in reaction to the fertility issue was not uncommon. For example, seeing other pregnant women or small children often caused feelings of guilt or grief. Menstruating was often associated with increased emotional pain. Conception subsequent to the abortion became a stressful time for many of the subjects. Failure to conceive or miscarriage was often related back to the abortion decision with a sense of guilt associated to the abortion. Once a pregnancy was underway, many women commented on their high degree of anxiety over fears of having a deformed child, a miscarriage, or other complications of pregnancy as a consequence of the abortion experience. This was often a mixture of legitimate health concerns regarding the status of their reproductive organs and religious concern over their fear of punishment from a retributive god.

For some women, experiencing a pregnancy following an abortion created a great deal of stress. Many of the subjects had dealt with the moral issue of whether or not their abortion involved taking a life by denying the existence of a human life at the time of the abortion. For the average woman in this sample, the abortion was performed at eleven and one-half weeks (the range was from six to twenty-four weeks). In subsequent pregnancies subjects often reported learning the details of embryonic and fetal development, which often caused a reappraisal of their earlier abortion decision. Attachment to the developing embryo that was to be carried to term often involved thoughts about the human potential and development of the aborted child. For many women this was a time of great stress, as it generated a great deal of guilt and grief. Pictures in particular, or graphic descriptions of the developing embryo, were likely to increase stress. These were inevitably encountered as the women read and prepared themselves for childbirth.

In addition to their individual stage in the human life cycle, the subjects were also members of families that were at particular stages in the family life cycle. For the majority of subjects the family-of-origin life stage was either launching or immediately post-launching. Many (27 percent) were still financially dependent on their parents, and even more (31 percent) lived with their families-of-origin. The remainder had been launched, although many were still struggling to establish themselves in new relationships or as singles. Seventy-two percent of the subjects were in steady relationships with the impregnating male partner, although few were married. Thus, for most subjects the pregnancy and abortion experience was at a time of transition when the family boundaries of the woman experiencing the pregnancy were not well defined. In most cases she was neither child nor spouse. This ambiguity of family boundaries (Boss, 1977) appeared to cause stress, as the abortion decision often included the task of clarifying family boundaries. Women who were financially dependent on their parents often mentioned family considerations as a primary reason for the abortion. They did not feel it was acceptable to bear a child or even admit pregnancy to their parents, as long as they were in the dependent status vis-a-vis their own parents. Their parents often concurred.

Unmarried subjects often clarified their family boundaries via the abortion decision. Between sexual partners, the decision to abort signalled the intent to keep the relationship on the same level of commitment, or a lesser degree, as opposed to becoming more committed. Often sexual relationships disintegrated soon after the abortion.

Economic Context

The economic context refers to the state of the larger environment's economy (Boss, 1985). The economic context of abortion was explored both in terms of the stress caused by the expense of the abortion and also in terms of the economic considerations taken into account when the decision to abort was made.

Although most subjects gave multiple reasons for deciding to have an abortion, economic considerations were raised by the majority of subjects. In most cases the decision to abort was not primarily based on economic considerations, although economics were used to strengthen the decision to abort once it was tentatively made. Subjects who wished to keep the child, but whose partners were unwilling to parent, often considered economics more seriously in their decision to abort. For these women it was often a case of having very little knowledge about what economic resources existed to support single parenting, rather than the absence of the resources themselves. Most subjects were unaware of the details of their eligibility for welfare benefits and charity had they decided to parent. Moreover, the decision to abort was made in the first or early second trimester before eligibility for many programs could begin.

The cost of obtaining an abortion was not prohibitive in any of the cases, although a number of the subjects were stressed by having to pay for the abortion in advance. One subject delayed obtaining verification of her pregnancy and subsequent abortion because she was unable to pay for these services. Her abortion was thus later term and a greater health risk. Another subject involved herself in a theft to obtain the money to pay for her abortion. Although some subjects were eligible to use health insurance to pay for their abortions, they elected not to in order to insure their anonymity. This created a greater financial burden. Many subjects were aided in paying for the abortion with funds from the impregnating male partner, although it was unusual for the partner to pay the whole amount.

Prices for abortion varied widely depending upon the year it was performed, the type of procedure, the weeks gestation, and the site where it was performed. For most subjects, paying for the abortion was not a major stressor, although for many it was a cause for concern.

Internal Contexts

The internal contexts in this model (Boss, 1985) are not independent of the external contexts, but rather serve as filters for those components of the external contexts the family and individual choose to include in their internal contexts. They are their philosophical, psychological, and sociological contexts. For example, the religious beliefs, cultural mores, and historical climate that are external to the family are filtered into it to determine the family's philosophical context or belief system. The internal psychological and sociological contexts are also influenced by what is present external to the family and the individual.

The internal contexts define how the individual or family has synthesized the external contexts into their own reality. From the results of this study, this section examines how abortion operates as a stressor on an individual level. This section will be followed by suggestions for further research, which is a necessary follow-up to the speculations and hypotheses generated from an exploratory study of this nature.

Sociological Context

The sociological context refers to the structure and function of the family regarding its boundaries, role assignments, and perceptions regarding who is in and who is outside of those boundaries (Boss, 1985). Boundary ambiguity is a major variable in this regard. Boundary ambiguity refers to an ambiguity between physical presence as opposed to psychological presence of a family member (Boss, 1977). In the case of abortion, ambiguous boundaries have a potential for causing stress.

Stress from abortion appears to be exacerbated when high boundary ambiguity exists. Boundary ambiguity in pregnancy results from a two-stage psychological process that occurs at different points along the continuum of pregnancy for different subjects. First, the physical presence of the pregnancy is acknowledged, either as a result of receiving a pregnancy diagnosis or from recognizing the signs of pregnancy.

Second, the pregnancy is recognized as having the potential for becoming a human infant who may or may not be admitted into the family boundaries. Recognition of the human potential of a pregnancy occurs for different subjects at varying times along the pregnancy continuum. It may occur simultaneously with the recognition of the physical fact of pregnancy or it may occur months later, even being delayed until the child is born. The point at which a pregnancy is perceived as taking on human form is highly dependent upon the cultural, religious, and historical contexts of an individual. Religious beliefs in particular may define for a woman when her pregnancy is to be recognized as having human form.

Pregnancy under many conditions is a time when a new family member is being psychologically admitted into the family and adjustments are being made as to how the family will be structured and function once the child arrives. This is a case where the family is functioning to psychologically recognize an infant that is physically present in pregnancy and soon to be born. Thus, boundary ambiguity is resolved when physical and psychological presence are congruent.

In the case of abortion, however, physical presence is being negated and thus incongruency and resultant boundary ambiguity will occur only if the psychological presence of the child is not also negated. This is not an issue for women whose abortions occur before they have psychologically recognized the pregnancy as having human form. However, for women who defined the pregnancy as having human form and subsequently decided to abort, there is the potential for boundary ambiguity to exist.

In these cases, boundary ambiguity exists when the psychological presence of the child does not diminish with the abortion. This occurred in this sample as was evidenced by the high degree of preoccupation with the aborted child reported by many subjects subsequent to their abortions. For these women, the psychological recognition of a child, albeit one that was aborted, was highly stressful. Guilt resulted over having denied the child life and membership in the family.

Efforts to repress or deny thoughts about the aborted child were mostly unsuccessful. Thus, resolution of the boundary ambiguity occurred in a curious fashion. Instead of diminishing the aborted child's psychological presence, it was increased. Children were given names, attributed characteristics (genetic traits and sex), and were fully admitted into the family, as the following quote illustrates:

> "There was no day that went by that I didn't think about that child. The baby would have been born at the end of August or the beginning of September. In all of my dreams I thought she would be a girl. And I named her. She is still so much a part of my life, even though I didn't choose to keep her."

As aborted children, they were recognized as non-physically present (i.e. dead) and grieved out of the family boundary in a manner that appeared similar to a normal grieving process. Thus, psychological presence and physical presence became congruent in a manner that allowed the subjects to grieve and resolve their guilt over the abortion.

Boundary ambiguity also occurred for subjects who did not recognize the pregnancy as having human form at the time of the abortion. For these subjects the boundary ambiguity occurred subsequent to the abortion and following a time period in which perceptions about the pregnancy were altered. Although the abortion was performed without reference to a potential human being, these subjects subsequently began to think of the pregnancy as having human form at the time of the pregnancy. Guilt and high psychological presence of the child resulted. Resolution of this form of boundary ambiguity occurred in a similar manner as described above.

Boundary ambiguity was enhanced by beliefs that defined the products of conception as having a "soul" or "afterlife." Beliefs that defined the soul of the fetus as living in a spiritual realm following the abortion were likely to contribute to a recognition of psychological or "spiritual" presence of the aborted child, and thus to boundary ambiguity. Stress appeared to be enhanced when beliefs in ensoulment were present. This was due to a concern over whether or not the abortion had denied the child's spirit entry into "heaven"; a right which is usually accomplished by baptism. Thus, some subjects reported baptizing the expulsed fetus, the blood leftover on the table, or their pregnant abdomens in an effort to ensure the fetus's spiritual rights.

Resolution of boundary ambiguity when beliefs in ensoulment were present differed from cases without these beliefs. Most notably, the subjects with such beliefs were likely to report experiences of some sort of visitation of the spiritual form of the aborted child. Usually this was a benign experience in which the spirit of the child was reported to reassure the subject regarding its well-being or to forgive her for the abortion. In only one case was the visitation perceived as a stress-enhancing experience. This occurred with a subject who had the experience of perceiving her aborted fetus crying out for her every night in an effort to recover its mother. In this case her guilt was greatly enhanced and she coped by drugging herself to sleep until the visitation experiences no longer occurred.

When boundary ambiguity occurred in relation to abortion, it appeared to be a major contributor to stress. Continued or new preoccupation with the aborted child, or spiritual visitations were very disturbing experiences that were not dismissed easily from consciousness. Thus, these subjects found themselves having to resolve the boundary ambiguity issue by increasing psychological recognition of the aborted child, which was also stressful as it necessitated a subsequent grief process. The inability to label this phenomenon or discuss it coherently with others was equally disturbing to subjects.

Many subjects felt, or received feedback from others that, having made the abortion decision, they had no right to ruminate about nor grieve the aborted child, thus the resolution process was often delayed, sometimes for years. This is illustrated by the following quote from a subject who felt that grieving for an aborted child was not a socially supported behavior:

"It is very difficult to talk to someone who is in the process of grief. She is mourning for her child. If she had a miscarriage she would be allowed to mourn for that child. But she is not allowed to mourn for that child if she had an abortion."

Being denied the right and support to grieve openly occurs also in the Jewish cultural context where stillborn babies are not generally accorded rites of mourning (Boss & Greenberg, 1984).

Guilt and conflicting feelings about the abortion appeared to be greatly relieved when the boundary ambiguity issue was resolved successfully through an increased recognition and subsequent grief process.

Psychological Context

The psychological context refers to the subject's ability (or inability) to use defense mechanisms when a stressful event occurs (Boss, 1985). Defense mechanisms were explored in the context of the subjects' coping strategies for dealing with the stress of abortion. As was anticipated, the use of repression and denial were of great importance. Not unlike many other samples of women who became pregnant, the women in this sample already used both repression and denial as a means of coping with their sexuality. Sexual guilt was allayed by denying to oneself and one's family that sexual activity was occurring. For a majority of the sample, this included a lack of use of consistent and reliable means of contraception. In comparison to other samples, this result indicating use of repression and denial was neither unexpected nor unusually out of proportion for women of this age group.

What is interesting is that many of these subjects continued to use repression and denial as primary coping strategies until their lives became so unmanageable that new means of coping had to be adopted. Thus, a great portion of the sample did not admit pregnancy until a pregnancy test could no longer be avoided without also jeopardizing their chances to obtain an abortion. Abortion was often engaged as a strategy for coping with the pregnancy without fully admitting that the pregnancy existed. Thus, for many of the subjects the decision-making period was not viewed as a time of decision, but as a time of panic during which they attempted to restore psychological equilibrium by denying through abortion that the pregnancy existed. Following the abortion, affect was suppressed by many of the subjects in order that the pregnancy and abortion could continue to be denied. Unfortunately, this demanded greater and greater psychological energy which resulted in having to drug oneself or enter social relationships that could support the denial (i.e. shallow sexual relationships or shallow friendships). This all too often resulted in a final psychological crisis in which the subject found herself suddenly confronted with her sexuality, her sexual behaviors, her pregnancy and her abortion, often years after all of these events had occurred. Thus, repression and denial were effective coping mechanisms to deal with sexual guilt in the time period prior to the pregnancy and immediately following the abortion, but they unfortunately did not function in the long term. That denial is a coping mechanism often useful in the short term but less functional in the long term has been noted by Boss (1985).

Projection was another defense mechanism that was often engaged. Rather than taking total responsibility for the abortion decision, many of the subjects reported blaming the abortion personnel for pushing them into the abortion. In some cases it was unclear whether or not actual coercion had occurred. Three subjects reported that they were not allowed to change their minds regarding the abortion immediately before it took place. They stated that they were forcibly held or tied to the operating table or drugged heavily when they attempted to stop the abortion procedure just prior to its taking place. Others felt they had received biased counselling by health care providers who stated that the pregnancy at the stage it was aborted was non-human. Others felt they had been coerced by health care providers who exaggerated the risks to the fetus of being deformed. Although all of these allegations may be true, it appeared that the subjects wanted to share responsibility for the abortion with others, most notably with the abortion personnel. Partners and parents were also blamed for the abortion decision, although this appeared more to be economic coercion or coercion regarding retaining family membership. Choosing to parent without the support of significant others may have made the abortion appear to be the only feasible course of action.

Philosophical Context

The philosophical context of the family refers to its values and beliefs on a micro-level. Individual rules of the family may be different from the culture in which they belong (Boss, 1985). One of the areas of exploration pertaining to philosophical context was the stated and implicit rules of the family pertaining to sexual behaviors and their outcomes. It became apparent in this sample that a major reason for abortion among these subjects was to protect the family paradigm (Reiss, 1981) or belief system concerning sexual behaviors. Subjects reported that abortion was considered necessary because the family-of-origin held rigidly to a set of beliefs that defined out-of-wedlock sexual activity as unacceptable. Pregnancy was not considered as unacceptable to one's parents as was the fact that it represented out-of-wedlock sexual activity. Thus, many of the subjects reported engaging in abortion as a means of protecting extended family relationships by preserving the family belief system.

The parental generation, more so than the sibling sub-system, was protected from challenge to the family paradigm. Thus, siblings were sometimes told of the pregnancy and abortion while very few parents were informed. The pregnancy and abortion experience were thus shared with few members of the family-of-origin and the abortion remained a family secret often up to and, one would assume, beyond the time of the interview. In some cases this secrecy involved family collusion. Subjects were aware that their parents knew or suspected the pregnancy and abortion had occurred, but all were in agreement about keeping it a subject not open for discussion.

Thus, family rules concerning sexual behaviors were very influential concerning how to cope with the pregnancy and to whom subjects could turn for support in dealing with the stress of their abortion experience. When subsequently stressed by their abortions, many subjects found themselves alienated from the family members they had tried to protect. These relationships became hurtful and the women withdrew from contacts with their family-of-origin, as it became too painful to be unable to share the grief and emotional reactions of the abortion with them.

CHAPTER 5
CONCLUSIONS

As a result of the present research, several important conclusions are derived. The high degree of boundary ambiguity that existed for many subjects following their abortions appears to relate to a high degree of stress. Preoccupation with the characteristics of the aborted child (experienced by 89 percent of the subjects), along with nightmares, flashbacks, hallucinations, and perceived visitations related to the abortion, were viewed in this research as indicators that subjects had a high degree of psychological presence regarding the aborted fetus. The boundary ambiguity and accompanying stress that occurred as an apparent result of this high psychological presence was resolved only when subjects began a grief process in regard to the aborted child. Although this grief process was often delayed, all of the subjects reported having one or more symptom of grief which occurred either immediately or in the long term.

Delays in the grief process appear to relate to the belief systems of subjects and their families-of-origin. Perceiving that their families-of-origin were likely to be highly stressed if told about the pregnancy, the majority of subjects kept their pregnancy and abortion experiences a secret from their families. Keeping the abortion a secret functioned as a means of protecting the family-of-origin belief system from challenge and thus preserving the subject's membership in her family-of-origin. However, keeping the abortion a secret required that subjects hide their feelings about the pregnancy and abortion which appears to have contributed to a high degree of isolation and alienation from the families-of-origin. It also occurred to a lesser degree in friendship systems, although the necessity to hide feelings about the abortion derived less from moral beliefs than from the perception that friends were unwilling to be confronted by the emotional reactions that may occur as a result of abortion.

The family-of-origin belief systems of many of the subjects also appear to have contributed to the use of denial and repression as major coping mechanisms. Family belief systems that opposed out-of-wedlock sexual intercourse and/or abortion appeared to contribute to the subjects' perceived need to keep their sexual behaviors hidden. This often extended to denial and repression on the individual level as evidenced by subjects' failure to use contraceptives (or use them effectively) because of their denial of the potential for pregnancy to occur. In many cases, subjects appear to have engaged in the abortion as a means of denying both to themselves and their families-of-origin that their out-of-wedlock sexual behaviors were occurring. After the abortion, continued denial and repression occurred regarding the emotional reactions to the abortion.

Denial and repression appear to have functioned as coping mechanisms in the short term, since they facilitated subjects' avoidance of emotional and family conflicts regarding sexual behaviors. In the long term, however, the use of denial and repression appears to have contributed to high stress reactions. The emotional reactions of subjects to the abortion experience were often too strong to repress, causing subjects to be confronted with their emotions and the behaviors that led up to them. This was often a very stressful experience.

The use of repression and denial to deal with sexual guilt became less effective in the long term as evidenced by the variety of symptoms reported by subjects, that appear to indicate guilt. The majority of subjects expressed a variety of fears about their apparent guilt over the abortion. These included fear that others would learn of the abortion, fear of punishment from a retributive god, and fear of future infertility. Many (69 percent) of the subjects reported becoming sexually inhibited and having feelings of sexual anxiety (35 percent) following their abortions. Many subjects reported feelings of discomfort around infants, small children, and pregnant women. A significant portion of the sample (23 percent) reported self-defined periods of anorexia nervosa that appear to have occurred as a result of the high stress following the abortion. The amenorhea that accompanies anorexia may have functioned, for these subjects, as an unconscious means of ensuring that another pregnancy and abortion experience would not occur. Subjects also reported attempts to repress their emotions concerning the abortion by increasing their use of drugs or alcohol. This in turn appears to have been related to suicidal thoughts and gestures. Fifty percent of the subjects reported subsequently becoming pregnant in reaction to the abortion. These subsequent pregnancies were often a means (as perceived by subjects) of checking their fertility and atoning for the abortion.

Many of the subjects found relief from their guilt concerning the abortion by turning to religion and their concept of god to obtain forgiveness, or by talking about the abortion to others who were accepting of the experience.

Although these findings have clarified how abortion functioned as a stressor in this sample, their generalizability to the population of aborters in general is limited. Further research is needed investigating the variables identified here and using more representative samples.

Areas of Future Research

The results of the present research are clearly limited in their applicability. It is not possible to generalize widely to the population of females in general from a sample of subjects selected on the basis of their perceptions of abortion as a stressful experience. There is a need to examine stressful abortion experiences using a larger more representative sample.

The results of this research have made clear that high psychological presence of the aborted fetus and the resultant boundary ambiguity are particularly related to stress following abortion. Future research will therefore need to investigate how the variable of boundary ambiguity and the grief process necessary to resolve high boundary ambiguity contributes to stress following abortion.

In addition, the influence of religious beliefs and belief systems in general on stress following abortion needs further examination. The use of denial and repression on the part of the subject in regard to sexual issues as a means of protecting the family-of-origin belief system and preserving membership in the family-of-origin, needs further clarification.

This research has also demonstrated that many of the indicators of stress following abortion do not appear until months or years after the abortion has taken place. Future childbearing, in particular, appears to be an event that triggers stress reactions. For that reason, the suggested format for future research regarding post-abortion stress is the longitudinal or cross-sectional design, which includes women who have had subsequent pregnancies.

The in-depth case study methodology of the present research made possible the collection of a great deal of qualitative data concerning stressful abortion experiences. The task of future research will be to develop instrumentation to collect this qualitative data in a manner that allows it to be quantified without compromising the nature of the data collection, and without being prohibitive in terms of cost for use with larger samples.

Future research that is able to estimate the percentage of women having abortions who are stressed by their abortion will be relevant to policy makers and clinicians. If such research is also able to make reliable estimates regarding the subject's potential for stress with given contextual characteristics, it may be possible to prevent and alleviate the stress of abortion for such women. This would be a great contribution to the body of research about abortion and its effects on women.

APPENDIX A
HUMAN SUBJECTS FORM

INTRODUCTION LETTER TO PROSPECTIVE SUBJECTS

Dear Friend,

I am a social scientist from the University of Minnesota. I am conducting research for my doctoral dissertation regarding the social-psychological outcomes of abortion. As you may be aware, abortion for some women is a very stressful process that continues to be stressful subsequent to the abortion. High stress reactions to abortion have not been well documented, are poorly understood, and are often not anticipated by the women who experience them. In order to help prevent and remediate the stressful effects abortion has in the lives of some women, these post-abortion stress reactions need to be better documented and understood.

I realize this may not be an easy time for you, but because of your experience you can be of help in a study of post-abortion stress reactions which I am conducting. Very little is known about how women react to abortion. It is my hope that the results of this study may be used to help prevent and remediate the stress that women may experience after abortion. A greater understanding of the stress that women may experience subsequent to abortion may be useful to those women who are at risk for high stress and to the clinicians who advise them.

You can help if you would be willing to take part in a private interview concerning your experience. What I will do if you agree to participate is contact you by telephone to arrange a time for us to talk. The interview may take place over the telephone for complete confidentiality or in person, if you prefer.

If you agree to participate, the interview will cover the circumstances under which you became pregnant, the decision-making process ending in abortion, the abortion experience, and your subsequent stress reactions to the abortion itself. The interview deals with a sensitive subject area which you may find somewhat stressful to talk about. If at any time before or during the interview you wish to discontinue the interview or withdraw from the study, you will be free to do so.

If you are willing to participate, please inform the person who gave you this description. Your first name only and telephone number will then be given to me and I will be contacting you shortly to arrange a time for the interview. If you prefer, you may of course feel free to contact me yourself.

If you have any questions please feel free to reach me at the following number (703) 820-1084.

Sincerely,

Anne Speckhard

APPENDIX B:
INTERVIEW SCHEDULE

Description of the Research to the Subject

Hello _____(subject's name)_____. This is Anne Speckhard. _____ gave me your name and phone number. She said you had agreed to take part in the research that I am conducting for my doctoral dissertation regarding the stress women experience after an abortion experience. Through interviews with women who have had stressful post-abortion experiences, I am trying to document the symptoms of their stress as well as the social context in which the pregnancy and abortion took place. Are you willing to take part in the interview?

The interview takes about forty-five minutes and it will be conducted over the phone (offer face-to-face for women in local areas). I am only interviewing women who considered their abortion experiences to be highly stressful. _____ said that you considered your abortion experience as highly stressful. Is that correct?

We can either schedule a time for the interview or, if you would like, the interview can take place right now. Which is better for you?

(At the time of interview)

The interview will cover the topics of your pregnancy and abortion experience, the social context in which it took place, and the stressful symptoms you may have experienced subsequent to the abortion. The interview deals with a sensitive subject and you should feel free to refuse or withdraw your consent at any time throughout the interview.

All of the information you provide will be treated with complete privacy and confidentiality. The write-up of the results will contain no information which could identify you. I will be happy to answer any questions you may have about the research and, if you wish, provide you a summary of the research results.

I would like to tape record this interview, if that is alright with you. The reason I'm taping is that I can't write as fast as you can talk, and it slows us down quite a bit if I take notes instead. If you allow me to tape record, I want you to know that the tape will be destroyed after a transcript is made of the interview. Do I have your permission to tape record? Okay, then I'll turn on the recorder and we can begin.

To begin the interview, I have found it helpful to let subjects begin by telling their own story in their own words before I ask a lot of questions. So if you would like to give me a summary of your pregnancy and abortion experience in your own words, that would be very helpful. You can begin with the circumstances under which you became pregnant, and include how the decision to abort was made, the experience of the abortion procedure, and the stressful symptoms you experienced after the abortion. Then I will follow up your account with questions on those topic areas that you didn't cover. That way you will be able to relate the experience in your own words and the sequence that makes most sense to you. Feel free to take as long as you like and include whatever you think is important. So, if you are ready, you can begin with the circumstances under which you became pregnant.

Follow-Up Questions:

What were your living arrangements at the time you became pregnant?

____ I was living alone
____ I was living with a female roommate(s)
____ I was living with my male partner
____ I was living with the family I grew up in
____ Other, please specify_____

What were your financial conditions at the time you became pregnant?

____ I was making a living and providing for myself
____ I was financially dependent on my parents
____ I was financially dependent on my male partner
____ I was financially dependent on the government (e.g., Welfare)
____ Other, please specify_____

What was your primary occupation at the time you became pregnant?

____ I was a high school student
____ I was a college student
____ I was working as a _____
____ I was primarily a mother
____ I was primarily a housewife
____ I was primarily unemployed

How old were you at the time you became pregnant? _____

How old was your male partner? _____

How long had you been in a relationship with the man who impregnated you?

____ Less than 2 weeks
____ Less than a month
____ One to three months
____ Three to six months

___ Six months to a year
___ One to two years
___ More than two years

What was your relationship like with the man who impregnated you?
___ It was a casual encounter
___ It was a steady relationship with no definite future commitments;
___ It was a steady relationship with informal commitments to the future

___ We were planning to marry
___ We were engaged to be married
___ We were married
___ The pregnancy was a result of an extra-marital affair (he was married ___, I was married ___, we were both married ___)
___ The pregnancy was a result of rape
___ The pregnancy was a result of incest

How long had your relationship with this man been sexually active?

___ Less than 2 weeks
___ Less than a month
___ One to three months
___ Three to six months
___ Six months to a year
___ One to two years
___ More than two years

Which, if any, birth control methods were you using at the time you became pregnant?

___ No birth control
___ Withdrawal
___ Douche
___ Foam
___ Diaphram

___ Condom
___ IUD
___ Pill
___ Rhythm (calendar method)
___ Natural family planning (Sympto-Thermal Method)

How would you characterize your feelings about the sexual relationship before you became pregnant?

___ The sexual relationship was mutually satisfying
___ I would have preferred not to be sexually active, but agreed to please my partner
___ My partner would have preferred not to be sexually active but agreed to please me

How would you characterize your feelings about a pregnancy before you became pregnant? (check all that apply)

___ I never thought about the possibility of a pregnancy
___ I welcomed the idea of a pregnancy because I thought
    ___ It would mean we could get married
    ___ It would help our relationship
    ___ I wanted a child
    ___ I wanted to test my partner's commitment to me
    ___ I wanted to be sure I could conceive
    ___ Other, please specify_____
___ I worried about what I would do if I became pregnant

In terms of your own feelings only, how would you classify this pregnancy? (check all that apply)

___ Wanted
___ Unwanted

___ Intended
___ Unintended

___ Contraceptive failure

When you first suspected you were pregnant what were your feelings (check all that apply)

	Not at all	Somewhat	Very
Afraid			
Sad			
Angry			
Happy			
Panic Rx.			

If you told your partner about the pregnancy what were his feelings as far as you know?

	Not at all	Somewhat	Very
Afraid			
Sad			
Angry			
Happy			
Panic Rx.			

If you told your partner about the pregnancy, what was his reaction? (check all that apply)

___ To support me in mutual decision-making
___ To take over and make the decision for me
___ To withdraw and leave me on my own to decide
___ To become violent
___ To become highly emotional and incapacitated
___ To ridicule me
___ To either abandon me or kick me out
___ Other, please specify_____

If you told your partner about the pregnancy, what was his recommendation?

___ Abortion
___ Adoption
___ Get married and keep the baby
___ Not get married, but keep the baby

If you did not tell your partner about the pregnancy, what were your reasons?

____ The relationship was ended before I was aware of the pregnancy

____ I was trying to protect myself from my partner's anger or rejection

____ I was trying to protect my partner from distress

____ I was afraid he would try to coerce me into an abortion

____ I was afraid he would try to coerce me into keeping the child

____ I expected him to be nonsupportive of any pregnancy resolution strategy

____ I thought if he knew about the pregnancy it would hurt our relationship

Have you ever told your partner about the abortion?

____ No ____ Yes

What happened to your relationship with the man who impregnated you?

____ It ended before the pregnancy was known

____ It ended as a result of the pregnancy

____ It ended as a result of the abortion

____ We eventually got married

____ Other, please specify_____

If you told your parent(s) about the pregnancy, what were their feelings? (check all that apply)

	Not at all	Somewhat	Very
Disappointed	_____	_____	_____
Afraid	_____	_____	_____
Sad	_____	_____	_____
Angry	_____	_____	_____
Happy	_____	_____	_____

If you told your parent(s) about the pregnancy, what was their reaction? (check all that apply)

____ To support me in mutual decision-making

___ To take over and make the decision for me
___ To withdraw and leave me on my own to decide
___ To become violent
___ To become highly emotional and incapacitated
___ To ridicule me
___ To either abandon me or kick me out
___ Other, please specify_____

If you told your parent(s) about the pregnancy what was their recommendation?

___ Abortion
___ Adoption
___ Get married and keep the baby
___ Don't get married but keep the baby

If you did not tell your parents about the pregnancy before the abortion, what were your reasons? (check all that apply)

___ I was trying to protect myself from their anger and rejection
___ I was trying to protect them from being hurt
___ I was afraid they would try to coerce me into keeping the child
___ I expected them to be nonsupportive of any pregnancy resolution strategy
___ They did not know I was sexually active and this knowledge would have hurt our relationship
___ Other, please specify_____

Have you ever told your parents? ___ No ___ Yes

If you had a pregnancy test to confirm your pregnancy, how pregnant were you at the time of the test? Circle the month and week of your pregnancy if you know it.

Weeks:	1	2	3	4	5	6	7	8	9	10	11	12	13	14
Months:				1				2				3		

Weeks:	15	16	17	18	19	20	21	22	23	24	25	26
Months:		4				5						6

Weeks:	27	28	29	30	31	32	33	34	35	36
Months:		7				8				9

If you delayed getting a pregnancy test, what were your reasons? (check all that apply)

___ There was no delay
___ I was afraid of the results
___ I didn't know where to go for a test
___ I was afraid others might find out
___ I did not even suspect that I was pregnant until quite late
___ Because I had irregular periods
___ Because I did not know the symptoms of pregnancy
___ Because of denial; I couldn't believe that I could be pregnant

At the time you received the pregnancy test and its results, were any of the following pregnancy resolution strategies presented to you by the health care providers? Check those that were presented as possible options.

___ Abortion
___ Adoption
___ Maternity home
___ Parenting

Did you feel urged by the health care providers to have an abortion?

___ Yes ___ Somewhat ___ No

If you believed your child might be defective in some way, what were your beliefs based on?

___ Results of amniocentesis test
___ Recommendation of doctor
___ Recommendation of abortion counselor
___ Other, please specify_____

What defect did you fear?

___ Defect due to my use of drugs or alcohol during pregnancy

___ Defect due to genetic abnormality
___ Defect due to viral infection (measles, etc.)
___ Other, please specify_____

Before the abortion, who did you talk with about the pregnancy? Check all that apply and the advice that was given, if any (e.g., abort, adopt, or parent) Advice:

                                                    Advice
___ My partner   _____
___ My parent(s)   _____
___ My sister(s) or brother(s)   _____
___ Other family members, please specify_____
___ My clergyperson   _____
___ Abortion personnel   _____
___ Counselor other than abortion counselor

                                        _____
___ Teacher   _____
___ Friends   _____
___ My doctor   _____
___ Other, please specify_____

Was there any time before the abortion that you wished to carry the baby to term either to parent or give it up for adoption?

___ Yes, the whole time
___ Yes, some of the time
___ Yes, briefly
___ No, never

If you felt forced into having an abortion, who was the forceful person(s)?

___ My mother
___ My father
___ My partner
___ The abortion personnel

If you were ambivalent about the decision to abort, what kept you from changing your decision?

____ It was never really my decision, I was coerced by others to abort

____ I had no support for keeping the baby

____ I was unaware of any resources or people that would have helped me if I had decided to keep the baby

If you were ambivalent about having an abortion, whose support would you have needed to keep you from having it done?

____ Any concerned party who would support my decision to carry the baby to term

____ My partner

____ My parents

____ Other, please specify_____

In the end, what were your reason(s) for the abortion? (check all that apply)

____ I wanted to hide the pregnancy from others

    ____ My parents

    ____ My partner

    ____ My friends

____ Pregnancy and parenting would interrupt my plans

____ I felt pressured by others to abort

____ I was afraid the child would be defective in some way

____ I was unwilling to parent without my partner's support

____ I was unwilling to feel that I had forced my partner to marry me

____ I felt unable to parent due to some deficiency on my part

    ____ Financially unable

    ____ Not mature enough to parent

    ____ Other, please specify_____

____ The pregnancy was a result of incest or rape

____ Other, please specify_____

How much time elapsed between the time you had your pregnancy confirmed by a pregnancy test and the time of the abortion?

____ The abortion was the same day

____ Less than 3 days

___ Less than a week
___ Less than two weeks
___ Two to four weeks
___ Four to six weeks
___ More than six weeks

Do you feel that there was sufficient time between the pregnancy test and the abortion for you to have made a well thought-out decision?

___ Yes, I had enough time
___ No, I was in a state of panic and did not have enough time to think clearly

Do you feel that the information you received about pregnancy resolution was adequate to base a decision upon?

___ Yes
___ Somewhat
___ No. If not, what was lacking?

In what city and state did the abortion take place? _____
_____

In what type of facility did the abortion take place?

___ Hospital, inpatient
___ Hospital, outpatient
___ Abortion clinic
___ Doctor's office
___ Other, please specify_____

Was the abortion ___ Legal, or ___ Illegal?

About how far did you have to travel to the abortion site? ___ miles

Who, if anyone, accompanied you to the abortion? (check all that apply)

_____ I was alone
_____ My partner
_____ My mother
_____ My sister
_____ My friend
_____ Other, please specify_____

How pregnant were you at the time of the abortion? Circle the month and week of your pregnancy if you know it.

Weeks: 1 2 3 4 5 6 7 8 9 10 11 12 13 14 15
Months: 1   2   3

Weeks: 16 17 18 19 20 21 22 23 24 25 26 27
Months: 4   5   6

Weeks: 28 29 30 31 32 33 34 35 36
Months: 7   8   9

What type of abortion counseling did you receive?

_____ Individual
_____ Group (If group, how many were in your group? _____

Did the abortion counseling address any of your fears or ambivalent feelings?

_____ Yes
_____ Somewhat
_____ No

Did the abortion counseling take place on the same day as the abortion?

_____ Yes
_____ No

Did you pay for the entire abortion procedure before you received abortion counseling?

_____ Yes
_____ No

Did you feel sure that you could at anytime before the actual abortion procedure began, change your mind, decide to leave and recover your fee?

___ Yes
___ Unsure
___ No

Once in the abortion clinic did you feel in charge of what was happening to you?

___ Yes, most of the time
___ Somewhat
___ No, not at all

Do you feel that the abortion counselor was honest with you and gave you complete information about the abortion procedure and its effects?

___ Yes
___ Somewhat
___ No

Do you feel that the abortion counseling adequately prepared you for what occurred during and after the abortion procedure?

___ Yes
___ Somewhat
___ No

What type of abortion procedure did you have?

___ Suction curettage or vacuum aspiration
___ Dilation and Curettage (D&C)
___ Saline injection
___ Prostaglandin Injection
___ Dilation and Evacuation (D&E)
___ Hysterotomy
___ Other, please specify_____

Did you at any time try to stop the abortion once it had begun?

___ Yes
___ No

If yes, what was the reaction of the staff?

What were your thoughts during the abortion procedure?

What were your feelings during the abortion procedure?

The next sections concern your social, emotional, psychological, behavioral and physical reactions to the abortion procedure. All of the symptoms listed are from reports of women who have had abortions or from the clinicians who cared for them. If we could go through the list of post-abortion symptoms and you could indicate which, if any, you experienced that would be helpful. Also, it would be helpful if, in indicating those symptoms you have experienced, you could indicate the duration of the symptom (for example, from the 2nd month to the 9th month after my abortion), its intensity from slight to moderate to severe, and, if any specific event or person triggered your reaction, please note that also. Please do not hesitate to list all of your symptoms, even if they seem odd to you. This will help a great deal in working with other women like yourself who have experienced similar events.

Affect Reactions

Duration	Intensity	Trigger	Feeling Reactions:
_____	_____	_____	Relief
_____	_____	_____	Happy
_____	_____	_____	Unburdened
_____	_____	_____	Sadness
_____	_____	_____	Grief

_____	_____	_____	Regret
_____	_____	_____	Sorrow
_____	_____	_____	Sense of Loss
_____	_____	_____	Numbness
_____	_____	_____	Shock
_____	_____	_____	Self Hatred
_____	_____	_____	Anxiety
_____	_____	_____	Paranoia that others will find out
_____	_____	_____	Fear of future infertility
_____	_____	_____	Fear that God would punish me
_____	_____	_____	Distrust of men
_____	_____	_____	Distrust of others
_____	_____	_____	Low self-worth
_____	_____	_____	Self-degradation
_____	_____	_____	Disappointment
_____	_____	_____	Self-doubt
_____	_____	_____	Ambivalence about the abortion
_____	_____	_____	Guilt
_____	_____	_____	Self-accusation
_____	_____	_____	Bitterness
_____	_____	_____	Victimized
_____	_____	_____	Anger
_____	_____	_____	Rage
_____	_____	_____	Hostility toward others
_____	_____	_____	Hurt
_____	_____	_____	Depression
_____	_____	_____	Hopeless
_____	_____	_____	Helpless
_____	_____	_____	Loneliness
_____	_____	_____	Nervousness
_____	_____	_____	Tension

			Sexual Phobia (Fear)
____	____	____	Feelings of craziness

Behavior Symptoms of Stress

Duration	Intensity	Trigger	Behaviorial Reactions
____	____	____	Crying
____	____	____	Decreased concentration
____	____	____	Nightmares
____	____	____	Insomnia
____	____	____	Hallucinations
____	____	____	Flashbacks of the abortion experience
____	____	____	Feeling haunted by the aborted child
____	____	____	Preoccupation with the age and characteristics the child would have had if it not been aborted
____	____	____	Discomfort around small children
____	____	____	Surprise at the intensity of my emotional reaction
____	____	____	Inability to communicate to others
____	____	____	Sexual inhibition
____	____	____	Deterioration of the sexual relationship with my partner
____	____	____	Break-up of the relationship with my partner
____	____	____	Sexual promiscuity

_____	_____	_____	A desire to make sure I am still fertile (able to have a baby)
_____	_____	_____	Repeat pregnancy
_____	_____	_____	Weight gain
_____	_____	_____	Weight loss
_____	_____	_____	Anorexia nervosa Bulimia
_____	_____	_____	Increased alcohol use
_____	_____	_____	Increased drug use
_____	_____	_____	Drug or alcohol addiction
_____	_____	_____	Suicidal thoughts
_____	_____	_____	Suicide attempts
_____	_____	_____	Loss of identity
_____	_____	_____	Lack of confidence in my ability to make decisions
_____	_____	_____	Distrust of self

After your abortion were you hospitalized for any reason that was connected to the abortion?

___ No
___ Yes

If yes, what was the reason? (check all that apply)
___ Physical complications of the abortion procedure
___ Psychiatric breakdown as a result of the abortion
___ Suicide attempt
___ Drug or alcohol addiction
___ Anorexia nervosa/Bulimia
___ Other, please specify_____

If your abortion included any medical complications, please describe them in as much detail as possible below. Include pain, infection, loss of reproductive capacity, and any other physical symptoms associated with your abortion.

If you had physical complications, where did you go for help?

____ Back to the abortionist
____ To my regular doctor
____ To the emergency room of a hospital
____ Other, please specify_____

If you required medical attention as a result of abortion complications, are you aware of whether or not your case was reported to the Center for Disease Control either by your doctor, the abortionist, whoever saw you, or yourself?

____ Yes, it was reported
____ Unsure
____ No, I'm sure it was not reported

Do you make a point of telling your ob/gyn or family practitioner or whoever takes care of you medically that you have had an abortion?

____ No, I have not told my doctor
____ I have not seen a doctor since my abortion, but
    ____ I do intend to tell
    ____ I do not intend to tell
____ Yes, I have told my doctor

As a result of your abortion experience, did you find yourself becoming isolated and alienated from others?

Yes Somewhat No
____ _____ ____ My friends
____ _____ ____ My parents
____ _____ ____ My partner
____ _____ ____ Other family members. Please specify.____
_____

If you experienced stress after your abortion, where did you go for help?

____ Return to the abortionist or abortion counselor
____ Psychotherapist
____ Medical doctor
____ Clergy
____ Friends
____ Family members
____ WEBA
____ Other, please specify_____

What were the most helpful things you did to cope with the stress that followed your abortion?

Before your abortion, did you have any history of psychiatric difficulties? If so, please specify.

____ No
____ Yes

Before your abortion what were your beliefs about abortion? (check all that apply)

____ I never really thought of it as a moral issue
____ I thought every woman ought to have the right to choose
____ I thought fetuses ought to have the right to life
____ I thought it was wrong except in circumstances where
    ____ the mother's life was endangered
    ____ the fetus was severely deformed
    ____ the pregnancy was the result of rape or incest
____ I thought it was murder under all circumstances

Now that you have had an aboration, what are your beliefs about abortion? (check all that apply)

____ I don't think of it as a moral issue
____ I think every woman ought to have the right to choose

___ I think fetuses ought to have the right to life
___ I think it is wrong except in circumstances where
   ___ the mother's life was endangered
   ___ the fetus was severely deformed
   ___ the pregnancy was the result of rape or incest
___ I think it is murder under all circumstances

What would you say your religious beliefs were at the time of the abortion and now?

Now At the time of the abortion

___ ___ I had no specific beliefs
___ ___ Jewish-liberal
___ ___ Jewish-conservative
___ ___ Mormon
___ ___ Catholic
___ ___ Episcopalean
___ ___ Methodist
___ ___ Lutheran-ALC, LCA
___ ___ Lutheran-MS, WS
___ ___ Fundamentalist Christian
___ ___ Born again Christian
___ ___ Other, please specify_____

At the time of the abortion, I would classify my parents', my friends', and my partners' beliefs as follows:

Parents	My Partner	My Friends	
_____	_____	_____	No specific religious beliefs
_____	_____	_____	Jewish-liberal
_____	_____	_____	Jewish-conservative
_____	_____	_____	Mormon
_____	_____	_____	Catholic
_____	_____	_____	Episcopalean
_____	_____	_____	Methodist
_____	_____	_____	Lutheran-ALC, LCA
_____	_____	_____	Lutheran-MS, WS

_____	_____	_____ Fundamentalist Christian
_____	_____	_____ Born again Christian
_____	_____	_____ Islam
_____	_____	_____ Buddhist
_____	_____	_____ Other, please specify____

What socio-economic status would you say you occupied at the time of your abortion?

___ Lower class
___ Low to middle class
___ Middle class
___ Mid to upper class
___ Upper class

What was your educational level at the time of the abortion?

___ Less than 8th grade
___ Less than high school
___ High school diploma or GED
___ Some higher education
___ Bachelor's degree in college
___ Graduate training beyond Bachelor's degree
___ Master or Ph.D. degree

What is your race?

___ White
___ Hispanic
___ Black
___ American Indian
___ Asian
___ Other, please specify_____

What is your predominant ethnic heritage? (e.g., Irish, Jewish, etc.)

Are you adopted? ___ Yes ___ No ___ Unsure

Is there anyone in your immediate or extended family that you know or suspect has been involved in an out-of-wedlock pregnancy or abortion? If so, please list their approximate age at the time of the pregnancy or abortion, their sex, and relationship to you. For example: My male cousin at age 15, my mother at age 40, my aunt and uncle at age 19.

Unmarried Preg.	Abortion	Relationship	Age

I have asked you a lot of questions and you have provided a lot of answers. Is there anything I missed that you might want to add at this point?

Is there any advice you have for other women contemplating abortion or experiencing stress after an abortion?

If you would like, I'd be pleased to send you a summary of the results of this survey. If so, I need you to fill out your name and address below. Of course, your name will never be included with any of your data and your answers will be kept completely confidential.

Name _____

Address _____

City/State/Zip Code _____

Telephone # _____

Would you be willing to take part in any further research on this topic? If so, please check here. ___ Yes ___ No

I would like to give you my name and telephone number as well, in case you have any questions or suggestions later on.

Lastly, if you know of anyone who has had a stressful post-abortion experience who might be willing to take part in this interview, I would appreciate your letting me know.

REFERENCES

American Jurisprudence of Facts. (1976) Informed consent laws.

Anonymous. (1979, Sept.-Nov.) Two women tell about their abortions. *Voice for the Preborn.*

Balter, S. (1962). The psychiatrist's role in therapuetic abortion: The unwitting accomplice. *American Journal of Psychiatry, 119,* 312-318.

Blumberg, B. D., Golbus, M. S., & Hanson, K. H. (1975). The psychological sequelae of abortion performed for a genetic indication. *American Journal of Obstetrics and Gynecology, 122,* 799-808.

Boss, P.G. (1985). Family stress: Perception and context. In M. B. Sussman and S. Steinmetz (Eds.), *Handbook on Marriage and the Family.* New York: Plenum Press.

Boss, P. G. (1977). A clarification of the concept of psychological father presence in families experiencing ambiguity of boundary. *Journal of Marriage and the Family, 39,* 141-151.

Boss, P. & Greenberg, J. (1984). Family boundary ambiguity: A new variable in stress theory. *Family Process, 23,* 543.

Bulfin, M. J. (1975, Oct.). *Deaths and Near Deaths with Legal Abortions.* Paper presented at the American College of Obstetricians and Gynecologists Convention.

Cvejic, H. (1977). Follow-up of 50 adolescent girls two years after abortion. *Canadian Medical Association Journal, 116,* 44-56.

Cowell, C. A. Problems of adolescent abortion. *Orthopanel 14,* Ortho Pharmaceutical Corporation Publication.

Friedman, C. M. (1974). The decision-making process and the outcome of therapuetic abortion. *American Journal of Psychiatry, 131,* 1332.

Hayasaka, Y. (1970, Oct.). *Japan's 22 Year Experience with a Liberal Abortion Law.* Paper presented at the XIIth International Congress of FIAMC.

Henshaw, S. K., Forrest, J. D., Sullivan, E., & Tietze, C. (1981). Abortion in the United States: 1978-1979. *Family Planning Perspectives, 13,* 6.

Henshaw, S. K., Forrest, J. D., Sullivan, E., & Tietze, C. (1982). Abortion services in the United States: 1979-1980. *Family Planning Perspectives, 14.*

Henshaw, S. K., & O'Reilly, K. (1983). Characteristics of abortion patients in the United States, 1979-1980. *Family Planning Perspectives, 15,* 5-16.

Hill, R., (1949). *Families Under Stress.* New York: Harper and Row. (Reprinted, Westport, Connecticut: Greenwood Press, 1971).

Kent, I., (1977, Sept.). *Emotional Sequelae of Therapuetic Abortion: A Comparative Study.* Paper presented to the annual meeting of the Canadian Psychiatric Association.

Kobb, L. C. (1958). *Abortion in the United States.* New York: Hoeber-Harper.

Luker, K., (1975). *Taking Chances: Abortion and the Decision Not to Contracept.* Berkeley: University of California Press.

Malmfors, K., (1958). The problem of women seeking abortion. In M. Calderone (Ed.), *Abortion in the United States* (pp. 133-135). New York: Harper & Row.

Osofsky, J. O., & Osofsky, H. J., (1972). The psychological reaction of patients to legalized abortion. *American Journal of Orthopsychiatry, 42,* 48-60.

Population Council. (1972). Joint program for the study of abortion (JSPA): Early medical complications of legal abortion. In C. Tietze and S. Lervit (Eds.), *Studies in Family Planning, 3.*

Reiss, D., (1981). *The Family's Construction of Reality.* Cambridge: Harvard University Press.

Roe v. Wade, Supreme Court decision, January 22, 1973.

Saltenberger, A. (1983). *Every Woman Has the Right to Know the Dangers of Legal Abortion.* Glassboro, New Jersey: Air Plus Enterprises.

Sands, W. L., (1973). Psychiatric history and mental status. In Freedman & Kaplan (Eds.), *Diagnosing Mental Illness: Evaluation in Psychiatry and Psychology* (p 31). New York: Atheneum.

Simon, N. M., & Sentuvia, A. G. (1966). Psychiatric sequelae of abortion. *Archives of General Psychiatry, 15,* 378-389.

Spaulding, J. G., & Cavenar, J. O., Jr., (1978) Psychoses following therapuetic abortion. *American Journal of Psychiatry, 135,* 364-365.

Zimmerman, M. K., (1977). *Passage through abortion: The Personal and Social Reality of Women's Experiences.* New York: Praeger Special Studies.